Usability Success Stories

Usability Success Stories

How Organizations Improve by Making Easier-to-Use Software and Web Sites

PAUL SHERMAN

Routledge
Taylor & Francis Group

LONDON AND NEW YORK

First published 2006 by Gower Publishing

Published 2016 by Routledge
2 Park Square, Milton Park, Abingdon, Oxon OX14 4RN
711 Third Avenue, New York, NY 10017, USA

Routledge is an imprint of the Taylor & Francis Group, an informa business

British Library Cataloguing in Publication Data
Usability success stories : how organizations improve by
   making easier-to-use software and web sites
    1.User interfaces (Computer systems) – Design 2.Web sites –
   Design 3.Human-computer interaction 4.Business – Data
   processing – Management 5.Computer software – Development –
   Human factors
   I.Sherman, Paul
   005.4'37

   ISBN 9780566086564 (hbk)

Library of Congress Cataloging-in-Publication Data
Usability success stories : how organizations improve by making easier-to-use software and web sites / edited by Paul Sherman
    p.com.
  Includes bibliographical references and index.
  ISBN-13: 978-0-566-08656-4 (alk. paper)
  ISBN-10: 0-566-08656-5 (alk. paper)
 1. New products--Management. 2. Customer relations. 3. User interfaces (Computer systems)
 I. Sherman, Paul, 1966-
  HF5415.15.U73 2006
  005.068--dc22

                                                        2006013672

Contents

List of Figures   *ix*
List of Tables   *xi*
Preface by Whitney Quesenbery   *xii*

Chapter 1   **An Introduction to Usability and User-Centred Design**
                 by Paul Sherman   **1**
                 Why write about successes?   2
                 The world of software development   5
                 User-centred design and usability engineering   7
                 Software development cultures   9
                 What we are going to talk about   11
                 Who should read this book?   12

Chapter 2   **Tracking Ease-of-Use Metrics: A Tried and True Method for**
                 Driving Adoption of UCD in Different Corporate Cultures
                 by Kaaren Hanson and Wendy Castleman   **15**
                 Introduction   15
                 The problem: representing the users in the development
                     process   16
                 The engineer-centric culture: we don't need all that fluff!   16
                 The design-centric culture: But it looks good!   18
                 The customer-centric culture: I know my customer!   19
                 The solution: ease-of-use metrics   20
                 The benefits of ease-of-use metrics   23
                 Establishing which areas of the product need more
                     resources/attention   29
                 Facilitating ROI calculations   30
                 How different cultures respond to ease-of-use metrics
                     and goals   31
                 Summary   37

Chapter 3   Tales from the Trenches: Getting Usability Through Corporate
              by Francis (Hank) Henry   41
              Gestating usability   41
              Besmirch the search   50
              Getting the user (customer) in front   54

Chapter 4   Redesigning the United States Department of Health and
              Human Services Web Site by Mary Frances Theofanos and
              Conrad Mulligan   63
              The process   63
              The content   64
              The politics   64
              Why redesign hhs.gov?   64
              Who redesigned hhs.gov?   66
              What we accomplished   67
              Drivers for the redesign   67
              Setting the stage: practical challenges to the E-Government
                regime   72
              The redesign process   74
              Lessons learned   83
              The content   84
              The politics   87
              Summary of outcomes   90
              One last lesson   91

Chapter 5   Creating Better Working Relationships in a User-Focused
              Organisation by Elizabeth Rosenzweig and Joel Ziff   93
              An example: starting with the best of intentions   96
              Analysis of the case study   105
              What we can do: resolving interpersonal impasses   105

Chapter 6   Using Innovation to Promote a User-Centred Design Process
              While Addressing Practical Constraints by Leslie G. Tudor
              and Julie Radford-Davenport   111
              What is Information Map Studio (IMS)?   111

The challenges 112

Overcoming the challenges: solutions within constraints 113

Summary and conclusions 132

Chapter 7 **Changing Perceptions: Getting the Business to Value**

User-Centred Design Processes by Adam Polansky **135**

Who am I to talk about this? 135

The vicious circle of distrust 137

A wink's as good as a nod to a blind man 138

The case study 139

The project parameter matrix 140

Feature value analysis 141

Feature and function identification 142

Feature/Function analysis 142

Quantifying the list 143

Contextual qualification 143

Horse trading 144

Site maps 145

'As-is' 147

'To be' 147

'To be later' 148

Wireframes 148

Built-in functionality 149

Why a success? 150

Chapter 8 **User Interface (UI) Design at Siemens Medical Solutions**

by Dirk Zimmermann and Jean Anderson **153**

Who we are and what we do 153

Structure of our product team 154

Exploring the medical domain, or why we leave user analysis

to the product analysts 156

Our process 159

How we got there 168

And where we want to go 174

Chapter 9   **Collaborating with Change Agents to Make a Better User**
                        Interface by Paul Sherman and Susan L. Hura   **177**

                   The situation   178

                   Let's do something about it   179

                   The analysis   180

                   The results   182

                   The pitch   185

                   The redesign   187

                   The outcomes   187

                   Lessons, helps and hindrances   188

Chapter 10   **Learning from Success Stories by Paul Sherman**   **191**

Index   *197*

List of Figures

Figure 2.1   The Ease-of-Use pyramid   22

Figure 2.2   Iterative process for meeting ease-of-use goals   23

Figure 2.3   Ease-of-use goals and success rates for three tasks   29

Figure 2.4   Ease-of-use metrics and indicators of UCD impact   32

Figure 3.1   Example search results page from jcpenney.com prior to
        redesign   51

Figure 4.1   Home page of hhs.gov before redesign   68

Figure 4.2   Home page of hhs.gov after redesign   68

Figure 4.3   The original HSS home page, with problems and
        issues highlighted   78

Figure 4.4   The redesigned HSS home page   82

Figure 4.5   Two visual treatments: informal (left) and formal (right)   83

Figure 5.1   A framework for situation assessment and action planning   95

Figure 5.2   Techniques for creating better working relationships   106

Figure 6.1   Sample slide used in the usability test report   121

Figure 6.2   Asynchronous collaborative design hallway display
        method   124

Figure 6.3   Asynchronous collaborative design rolling whiteboard
        display method   127

Figure 6.4   Design by appointment display method   129

Figure 7.1   Project parameter matrix   141

Figure 7.2   Site map   145

Figure 7.3   Site map detail   146

Figure 7.4   An example of a wireframe   148

Figure 8.1   The product development cycle at Siemens
        Medical Solutions   155

Figure 8.2   Layers of standards   156

Figure 8.3   Action-planning and execution matrix   161

Figure 8.4   A sample high-level navigation model   163

Figure 8.5   The Seven Steps to UI happiness   164

Figure 8.6   An interaction diagram involving integrated use of a web application and a medical device   165

List of Tables

Table 4.1   Success rates on usability test tasks, before and after site
             redesign   69

Table 4.2   Success rates for five baseline test scenarios   77

Table 6.1   Usability improvements for selected IMS tasks   118

Table 6.2   Advantages of the asynchronous collaborative
             design method   125

Table 6.3   Advantages and disadvantages of different asynchronous
             collaborative design techniques   130

Table 9.1   Issues identified and heuristic violated   183

Preface

User-centred design is based on one core idea: that the best way to create great products is to start by understanding the people who will use them, what they will use them for and how they will use them, and to use those insights to drive the design.

Simple, right? Maybe not.

When I was a very young practitioner, and full of enthusiasm for the power of user-centred design, I gave a presentation to the software development team for a Wall Street investment firm. When I finished, one of the managers challengingly asked, 'Isn't this just common sense?' The question took the wind out of my sails for a minute. After all, every one of their users worked within a few minutes' walk from the room where we sat. Maybe they were user-centred without knowing it. 'Sure,' I replied, 'but are you doing it?'

And that's the difficulty. It may be common sense, but we're not actually doing it, at least not often enough.

No one really argues that good information about customers – a deep understanding of how, when and why a product will be used, an analysis of user 'personalities' and behaviour, and the chance to evaluate a product *before* it is released – won't create better products. The question, then, is why isn't user-centred design a routine part of *every* product development project?

Over the years, advocates have pointed to more-successful design, higher profitability, lower costs, increases in productivity and the high moral ground as reasons to adopt user-centred design. Although logical arguments like these may work in individual discussions, they have failed to produce a groundswell of wide adoption.

Steve Denning, the master of corporate storytelling, might have the answer. He suggests that you can't predictably change the opinion of many people with appeals to logic, especially when you are suggesting a whole new approach. He argues that the only effective solution is to engage their imagination. By using stories that show how things might be, you can invite listeners in, asking them to envision themselves as participants in that story. They will fill in the blanks with their own perspectives and needs. In doing so, the dynamic will change from a discussion that triggers an instinctive defensive reaction to a shared vision of a better future.

What Paul Sherman has done in this book is gather stories from companies who are 'doing it' and seeing positive results of their commitment to user-centred design. These stories are told through the eyes of practitioners, and focus on not just what they did, but how they adapted to the specific projects on which they found themselves working. These are not glossy celebrations of a great product design, but stories of the journey it took to create success.

The common thread in these stories is the need to listen carefully for organisational requirements and issues. Each describes an approach that seems to arise almost naturally from the business context. When you read these stories, they may seem easy. But read them again, and you will see that they all start with careful listening and empathy and a clear analysis of the needs of their colleagues.

It's a user-centred approach to introducing user-centred design.

We need more of it. This means setting clear goals for usability to meet user needs, but also looking at how they support the company goals and strategy. It means evaluating success, for everyone, against those agreed-on metrics. It doesn't mean watering down your methodology or compromising on techniques, but finding the language that communicates most effectively.

It also means looking at the whole organisation, not just the user-centred design team of user researchers, interaction designers, information architects and usability engineers. Because for user-centred design to succeed, everyone has to contribute, in their own way: managers, with direction, schedule and budget; departments such as sales, service and training, which have direct user contact, with their insights into the market; development and IT with choices of technology and quality methods. Most importantly, it means ensuring that everyone who contributes is acknowledged and rewarded for their work.

As valuable as this book will be in introducing user-centred design to managers, developers and other colleagues, it will be equally valuable in helping those of us in the profession to see new ways to be advocates.

As you read these stories, think about your work and your company. Can you see it reflected in one of the chapters? Put a bookmark in it. Close the book. Now imagine the story that you want tell about how your current project became a success.

Whitney Quesenbery,
WQusability.com

CHAPTER 1

An Introduction to Usability and User-Centred Design

Paul Sherman

Have you ever struggled to figure out the remote for your new television or cable box? Do you often find yourself cursing at the airline's voice recognition system when you call to make a flight reservation? Have you ever become so frustrated with a computer application, web site or handheld device that you felt your blood pressure rising and your hands balling into fists?

Us too. That's why we wrote this book.

There's an entire profession – we call ourselves usability engineers, user experience designers, interaction designers, user-centred design practitioners and so on – that strives to eliminate these daily moments of frustration. Often it feels like an uphill battle. New technology is often fun and interesting. It sometimes delights us unexpectedly by solving some of life's little problems.

But the downside of new technology is that it's often designed by technologists. They regard new gadgets and devices as challenges to be mastered – and their designs reflect this mindset. In contrast, ordinary people often see new technology as a speed bump on the path of daily life. One more thing to devote scarce time and attention to. To the ordinary person, new technology can be powerful yet difficult to grasp; comprehensive and incomprehensible; robust yet obscure.

Because the technologists bring such wondrous things into existence, sometimes with nothing more than mysterious lines of symbols and numbers, organisations tend to let them exercise control over how ordinary people should interact with their creations.

But the technologists don't think like ordinary people. Even if they did, the very fact that they are so close to the details of their creations causes their understanding of them to differ radically from anyone else's understanding.

Remember, the 'ordinary person' we're talking about is your grandmother, your electrician, the school student at the supermarket checkout. Most people have the *capacity* to eventually understand a piece of technology at a comparable level of detail. But they don't have the *time* to learn the technology, much less the motivation. They're busy with other things.

Yet, time after time, organisations bring to market products that reflect the technologist's way of thinking. These are the devices, web sites and applications that raise our blood pressure.

The members of our profession are devoted to the never-ending task of minimising or eliminating these mismatches between technology's designers and its users. Often our efforts fall short. It's *hard* to shake the status quo in organisations that are so focused on technological innovation.

However, our profession increasingly gains traction. We learn how to influence the product managers who guide the creation of new technologies, the technologists who create them, the project managers who own the schedules and the executives whose decisions affect the dozens – sometimes hundreds – of people who contribute to the creation of new technologies.

This book is a place where you'll learn not only what contributors in our field do, but also how several of us have effectively influenced our organisations and got them to incorporate users into product design and development processes. You'll hear how we've convinced decision-makers in our organisations that listening to, watching and interacting with ordinary people as they attempt to use our creations increases acceptance of new technologies and helps the organisation achieve its financial goals.

WHY WRITE ABOUT SUCCESSES?

People spend increasing amounts of time and effort interacting with complex hardware and software products. In the future more, not less, technology will be introduced into our work and personal routines.

Some of the applications and products we interact with – such as airline check-in kiosks and ATMs – are easy to learn and easy to remember. Some are even a pleasure to use (think Apple's iPod, or virtually all of Google's offerings).

Others are hard to learn and hard to use, and in general frustrate us at almost every turn. When we encounter these products, we say they are not *user-friendly*, or that they are not very *usable*. Another way of saying it is that these products possess low (or poor) *usability*.

While there are nearly as many definitions of usability as there are usability practitioners, a concise definition can be found in the ISO standards (ISO 9241–11, 1998). The standards body defines usability as the effectiveness, efficiency and satisfaction with which a specific set of users can complete a specific set of tasks in a particular environment (Sherman and Quesenbery, 2005).

Hopefully, you noticed the focus on *the user* in that definition. This is no accident. Usability is all about *people*, not products. There is no 'objective' measure of usability that can be applied to any given device or application. The bottom line is this: if the intended users can use the product to accomplish their goals, then the product is usable. If they can't (or can't readily) use the product to accomplish their goals, then it's not really usable.

In our personal lives, products with poor usability cost us time and energy. How many times have you pushed a door handle instead of pulled, pressed 'Cancel' instead of 'OK', or sat seething in front of your computer monitor, unable to figure out how to purchase an item from an online retailer?

In the work arena, organisations also incur costs when people choose to (or are told to) use a product with poor usability. Businesses lose money because frustrated customers leave (Kehoe, Pitkow, Sutton, Aggarwal and Rogers, 1999). Productivity and even employee satisfaction decrease when employees use software applications with poor usability (Macleod, Bowden, Bevan, and Curson, 1997; Rehman, 2000).

Whether a product is used at work or at home, poor usability imposes significant costs on the producer of the product as well. Companies that make hard-to-use products incur higher support costs, spend more time and money on rework and tend to have less-satisfied customers (Bias and Mayhew, 1994; Wiklund, 1994).

These outcomes can be mitigated – and often avoided entirely – by applying a user-centred design process and usability engineering techniques during product development.

The discipline of user-centred design includes a set of techniques that help development teams accurately gather and assess target users' characteristics, goals and motivations, as well as their workflow, pain points and critical behaviours. User-centred design and usability professionals do things such as:

- watch people as they perform tasks and activities that product or service providers would like to assist, expedite or automate;

- discover people's skills, goals, motivations, frustrations and successes as they work (or play, or interact, etc.);

- create designs that assist, expedite or automate, with attention to the intended users' skills, goals, etc.;

- test these designs by having *people from the intended user group* attempt to perform the tasks and activities supported by the product;

- revise the design as necessary, on the basis of the results of the test sessions.

Armed with this knowledge, user-centred design practitioners are able to design features and interactions that meet the needs of the intended users.

Performing these activities costs both time and money to the organisation, but the costs of usability engineering are usually outweighed by the benefits. In some cases the benefits dramatically outweigh the costs, yielding surprisingly large economic rewards for organisations. Studies have been published documenting a tenfold return, and more, on investment for usability engineering activities (Bias and Mayhew, 1994; see also Lund, 1997).

Despite the evidence for a positive return on investment for usability engineering activities, many organisations view usability engineering as a 'nice to have', a non-critical part of the product development process. When times get tough, organisations routinely jettison their user-centred designers and usability engineers, if not during the first round of lay-offs then usually by the second or third.

It's apparent that the message doesn't always get through. In many cases the 'business' (shorthand for the portion of the organisation that decides what to build) and 'development' (the people who actually build what the business wants to build) do not recognise that dollars spent on user-centred design are dollars incredibly well spent.

The contributors to this book seek to change this by relating cases where user-centred design or usability engineering contributed significantly to the solution of a business problem. The authors also discuss organisational factors that facilitated or impeded the application of usability engineering to the problem. By telling their stories, the authors hope to accomplish two things:

- provide other practitioners with the benefit of their learning and experience, and

- demonstrate to technologists and business stakeholders the benefits of integrating user-centred design into their processes.

Why tell 'success stories'? The answer is deceptively simple: humans are drawn to narratives. The story is the oldest – and probably still the most effective – way to convey information. By using this format, we explicitly acknowledge and seek to leverage the power of narrative.

Before we tell our stories, here's some background on the strange world of software development, and more about usability and user-centred design.

THE WORLD OF SOFTWARE DEVELOPMENT

For those who have not witnessed it first-hand, the software development environment is an odd place. If you took a peek into a software development shop, you would be hard-pressed to see anything actually getting done. The product is created, lines of code at a time, across many software developers' computer systems. Each developer's pieces of code are compiled into 'builds' which represent a collection of executable code, code libraries, scripts and other digital objects.

If the build 'breaks' – that is, if it doesn't compile, the program doesn't run or it runs incorrectly – it's up to the testing group (known as Quality Assurance, or QA) to help identify the source of the breakage, document it and send the whole mess back to the software developers so they can fix the bugs. When enough bugs are fixed (or when time runs out and it's time to launch the product), the development efforts cease – at least for a while, until the next release kicks off, or the release is so buggy that a 'service release' (or 'patch') is necessary.

But this process represents only a piece of the picture. Many activities must take place before the developers start coding and QA starts testing. The most important activity that occurs is that *someone* decides what to build. Typically, the product management group – the 'business' – studies the market, the competition and various economic factors, and decides to build a product (or additional features for an existing product) that they believe will satisfy potential customers and meet the economic goals of the organisation. This is often referred to as the 'ideation phase'.

During this phase, the product manager (or in some organisations, the business analyst) begins to communicate with the software development group in a variety of informal and formal ways. Informally, they meet to discuss strategic directions and what features to build to attain the short-term and long-term goals of the business. More formally, product managers and business analysts produce and distribute *market requirements* or *business requirements* documents.

These documents typically describe the business case, or the justification for building the feature or product. They can also describe *what* the product or feature should do, typically in very granular, unitised statements known as *feature requirements*. In most software development organisations, these requirements documents are the 'spec' – the specification of what should be built by the development team.

Ideally, product management has a complete and thorough understanding of the potential customers' needs, and the requirements they write are unambiguous. That is, the requirements should be a faithful reflection of existing and potential customers' needs, and everyone who reads them should come away with the same understanding of the writer's intent.

In practice, neither of these objectives is attained with any degree of regularity. Usually two phenomena occur to prevent them:

- Product managers develop an inaccurate or impoverished understanding of the customers and their needs, and so the requirement set does not represent users' needs accurately, or represents them only incompletely (sometimes both).

- Software development attains an inaccurate or incomplete understanding of product management's intent, and so develops a feature or product that does not meet users' needs.

And when the product makes it to the marketplace, it ends up disappointing the customers.

Of course there is no perfect world; errors always creep into any human endeavour. But this particular state of affairs plays out time after time, project after project. There is no magic bullet to prevent these phenomena from ever happening, but there are techniques and methods to ameliorate and reduce their influence.

User-centred design and usability engineering are two of these methods.

USER-CENTRED DESIGN AND USABILITY ENGINEERING

Into this breach step user-centred design (UCD) and usability engineering. UCD and usability engineering employ observational and quasi-experimental methods to gather and assess target users' characteristics, goals and motivations; and document their workflow, pain points and critical behaviours.

This information is extremely helpful to the product manager or business analyst. One challenge they typically face is integrating population-level information such as market size, overall market trends and large sample surveys with their anecdotal encounters of small numbers of potential customers, often in focus group environments rather than in their place of business.

The notion that valuable information can be extracted from simply *watching* people as they work is simple yet powerful. Every – and I mean *every* – product manager and business analyst who has taken part in observational research sings the praises of the method (and often praises the USD practitioners as well!)

Why? Because observational research provides them with a rich set of actionable data. The data we collect describe *how* the target users currently solve their problems and attain their objectives, and *what* they do with prototypes or mock-ups of the proposed product. This offers product managers a means to bridge the gap between market-level quantitative data and their anecdotal experiences.

When people performing ideation-phase work are able to take part in methodologically sound observational research, the quality of their output invariably improves. They write better, more-complete, more-accurate requirements. And they carry in their heads a deeper understanding of their users. They draw on this understanding in their countless informal interactions with the developers and senior management.

User-centred design practitioners often have prototyping skills, meaning that they can mock up a product or feature. Even though prototypes and mock-ups can't be used as real products, their appearance and behaviour help the business more effectively convey their intentions and objectives to the developers, augmenting the written requirements documents. I have personally witnessed many a developer ask for a mock-up of a screen so they can better understand the requirements. Requirements are a useful tool, but for very complex designs they often fail to convey the 'big picture' intended by the requirements writer.

Finally, user-centred design practitioners and usability analysts are able to test prototypes of products and features – or early versions as they are built by the developers – with participants drawn from the target customer population. This affords the business the opportunity to see their solutions in action (albeit in a somewhat artificial 'lab' environment), and to assess where their requirements may have missed the mark.

The usability test setting also gives development the opportunity to assess whether their interpretation of the requirements – that is, their implementation – is on target. Development organisations often grow to appreciate usability engineers because they help development to implement the business vision more accurately.

So if everyone loves UCD and usability engineering, what's the problem? Why write this book?

We're telling our stories because, despite the seemingly obvious benefits conveyed by user-centred design and usability engineering, UCD practitioners are still not well integrated into product management and development organisations.

Many organisations struggle to determine how to incorporate user-centred designers, usability analysts and their methods into existing processes. And UCD practitioners often struggle to find ways to engage more effectively with the business and development, and accurately convey the value they can bring to the organisation. Why? Because organisational cultures – and the subcultures within them – change slowly, and only with persistent effort on the part of change agents.

SOFTWARE DEVELOPMENT CULTURES

The disciplines described above are not simply functions filled by interchangeable individuals. They represent sub-cultures within a larger organisational culture.

At the national level, culture can be defined as the way a group of people live their lives – the attitudes, values, behaviours and customs that reflect a group's approaches to surviving and thriving (Meshkati, 1994). Geert Hofstede calls national culture 'the software of the mind' (1991), drawing a parallel between a computer's operating system and the 'mental programming' of people within a culture.

Cultures also exist at the level of regions (think of the differences between areas of the USA), ethnic backgrounds, religious affiliations and vocational and educational choices. It should be obvious that we are all members of many different cultures simultaneously. Cultures overlap. So do their influences on people. Each culture exerts some effect on our attitudes, opinions, motivations and behaviours. Depending on the particular situation, a person's national, regional, ethnic or professional culture may be called into play, or 'activated' in response to some external stimulus.

Organisational culture and its effect on the people within organisations have been widely studied. (Hofstede, 1991; Ritchie, 2000; Driskill and Brenton, 2005). One interesting aspect of this subject area is how people's vocational, academic or professional cultures affect their interactions with people from other disciplines, and how differences and similarities across sub-cultures shape the formal and informal processes guiding the creation of products and services.

How do different cultures interact in the workplace? Sometimes with difficulty. In businesses that produce products or services, different disciplines – representing different cultures – are arrayed in ways that lead to inherent – in fact, necessary – conflict. The business wants to build more than developers' capacity allows. Developers want more time to build complex features; the business wants to allocate less. QA identifies a defect and tags it 'severe'; development thinks it's a minor or moderate bug. And they'd rather publish a workaround and fix it in Release 1.1. These conflicts are built into the process; they exist to help ensure products address people's wants and needs, make it to the marketplace on time, and possess sufficient quality.

In addition to the designed-in conflicts, there is conflict that is brought about by differences between disciplines in their members' technical background, training, and problem solving. Developers and QA analysts are typically trained in engineering or the hard sciences. The product managers are typically trained in economics, business or finance. Now add UCD to this mix. Some of us are trained in psychology, some in library sciences. Some have no formal training, just a love of the work and experience borne of on-the-job training.

These different disciplines usually have differing ways of communicating, thinking about issues, approaching problems and resolving conflict. So how does anything get done in this techno-Tower of Babel?

In every organisation there are individuals who break down the barriers between disciplines. They do this by building relationships with people in neighbouring disciplines, serving as translators, helping the members of each small sub-culture to remain focused on the overarching goals:

- Get the product out the door.

- Satisfy as many of the users' wants and needs as possible.

- Minimise the number and severity of defects in the product.

- Sell enough of a product to justify another release.

In Chapter 7, Adam Polansky calls these people the 'natural liaisons' in the organisation. Ideally, everyone in an organisation would function as a natural liaison. In reality, it seems that there are a small number of natural liaisons in each sub-culture. But the weight of the organisation is disproportionately borne by these individuals. The success of most initiatives can usually be traced back to the efforts of the natural liaisons as they communicated across discipline boundaries, forged relationships and shared understandings, and consistently went beyond the tasks depicted in their job descriptions.

If you haven't figured it out yet, let me state it outright: user-centred design initiatives don't succeed simply because practitioners know how to design a user research protocol or a usability test. UCD initiatives succeed in organisations because its practitioners and proponents also become liaisons across disciplines and to executive management. They learn to speak the languages of business and technology, and they communicate the value of UCD in terms that their counterparts understand. Most importantly, they *listen* to the concerns of the business stakeholders and the developers, and learn to frame their contributions in ways that demonstrate the power of user-centred design to solve business problems.

WHAT WE ARE GOING TO TALK ABOUT

The primary objective of this work is to relate instances where practitioners working within an organisation helped solve a business problem with UCD or usability engineering techniques, and made significant contributions to their organisation.

Our other objective is to discuss the organisational settings within which these successes were achieved, and provide the reader with an understanding of how user-centred design can be best organised and executed within a business. The authors describe the organisational barriers that were overcome, as well as the organisational factors that helped foster the conditions for the accomplishments.

- In Chapter 2, Kaaren Hanson and Wendy Castleman describe their experiences at Remedy Software, Peregrine Systems and Intuit, the makers of QuickBooks and TurboTax. At these companies they developed 'ease-of-use' metrics and used them to integrate UCD and usability engineering processes more tightly into their product management and development organisations.

- Hank Henry describes in Chapter 3 how a small team at the retailing giant JCPenney employed usability engineering techniques to point out deficiencies in the company's online experience, and advocated user-focused improvements to the jcpenney.com web site.

- Mary Theofanos and Conrad Mulligan tell their story (Chapter 4) about how user-centred design and usability engineering helped the US Department of Health and Human Services to redesign their web site to better meet the needs of multiple user groups, including members of the general public seeking health information; doctors, nurses, administrators and allied health workers; and others.

- Elizabeth Rosenzweig and Joel Ziff relate a case study in Chapter 5 of a home page redesign for the sales site of a major consumer electronics manufacturer. They use it to explore the interpersonal dynamics that play out between business stakeholders, technologists and UCD practitioners.

- In Chapter 6, Leslie Tudor and Julie Radford-Davenport relate how they persuaded their management and the developers at SAS to study the target users and expose them to prototypes of a business intelligence application, before releasing the product into the marketplace.

- You'll learn from Adam Polansky in Chapter 7 about a sub-discipline within the user experience field called information architecture, and how it was used by his organisation to redesign the web site for an international entertainment production company, on time and on budget.

- Dirk Zimmermann and Jean Anderson in Chapter 8 explain how they persuaded business stakeholders and development at Siemens Medical Solutions to re-engineer the design and development processes and achieved an increased focus on users. They also describe the organisational factors that aided – and impeded – the changes they implemented.

- In Chapter 9 Susan Hura and I describe our experience applying UCD methods to redesign the technical support line for the users of a professional tax preparation software application, and how the project grew out of a relationship formed between the user-centred design staff and the practitioners of Six Sigma, a set of process improvement methods based on rigorous statistical analysis.

Taken together, this information should provide you with compelling accounts of how user-centred design and usability techniques can be used to solve business problems, and a better understanding of the organisational factors that help – and hinder – the integration of UCD into existing processes and organisational structures.

WHO SHOULD READ THIS BOOK?

If you're an experienced usability engineer, a user-centred design practitioner, or a manager of engineers and practitioners, you will probably find these stories somewhat interesting. They may also provide you with some insight into the organisational cultures that you work within. But in these chapters you will probably not encounter unfamiliar methods or techniques. That's because we didn't create this book primarily for our peers.

We are mainly interested in reaching two groups of people:

- Those individuals who work within neighbouring disciplines such as product management, project management and software engineering.

- People who have risen to high positions within organisations who may have heard about usability, but aren't sure how it can be best deployed in their own organisation.

REFERENCES

Bias, R., and Mayhew, D. (1994). *Cost-Justifying Usability*. San Diego, CA: Academic Press.

Driskill, G.W., and Brenton, A.L. (2005). *Organizational Culture in Action: A Cultural Analysis Workbook*. Thousand Oaks, CA: Sage Publications, Inc.

Kehoe, C., Pitkow, J., Sutton, K., Aggarwal, G., and Rogers, J.D. (1999). *Results of GVU's Tenth World Wide Web User Survey*. Atlanta, GA: Graphics Visualization and Usability Center, College of Computing, Georgia Institute of Technology. (www.gvu.gatech.edu/user_surveys/survey-1998–10/tenthreport.html)

Hofstede, G. (1991). *Cultures and Organizations: Software of the Mind*. Maidenhead, U.K: McGraw-Hill.

ISO 9241–11. (1998). *Ergonomic Requirements for Office Work with Visual Display Terminals (Vdts) – Part 11: Guidance on Usability*. Geneva, Switzerland: International Organization for Standardisation.

Lund, A.M. (1997). *Another Approach to Justifying the Cost of Usability*. Interactions, 4, 48–56.

Macleod, M., Bowden, R., Bevan, N. and Curson, I. (1997). *The Music Performance Measurement Method*. Behaviour and Information Technology, 16, 279–293.

Meshkati, N. (1994). *Cross-Cultural Issues in the Transfer of Technology: Implications for Aviation Safety*. Report of the International Civil Aviation Organization Flight Safety and Human Factors Regional Seminar and Workshop (pp. 116–137). Amsterdam: The Netherlands.

Rehman, A. (2000). *Holiday 2000 E-commerce: Avoiding $14 Billion in 'Silent Losses.'* NY, NY: Creative Good.

Ritchie, M. (2000). *Organizational Culture: An Examination of its Effects on the Internalization Process and Member Performance*. Southern Business Review, 25, 1–6.

Sherman, P.J., and Quesenbery, W. (2005). *Engineering the User Experience: UX and the Usability Professionals' Association*. Interactions 12, 38–40.

Wiklund, M. (1994). *Usability In Practice: How Companies Develop User-Friendly Products*. Boston, MA: Academic Press.

CHAPTER 2

Tracking Ease-of-Use Metrics: A Tried and True Method for Driving Adoption of UCD in Different Corporate Cultures

Kaaren Hanson and Wendy Castleman

Do you want your company to use a user-centred design (UCD) process but aren't sure how to convince people of the value and impact a user experience group can have? Or, are you trying to justify growing your design and research team? This chapter describes methods we used in different corporate cultures to drive adoption of user-centred design.

INTRODUCTION

This book is a source of real-world case studies – usability success stories – that demonstrate the impact a user experience group can have on a company and its products. However, this chapter is not so much a single usability case study as a description of how we have successfully used 'ease-of-use' metrics[1] to change company cultures and improve both product usability and the bottom line. We use examples from Peregrine Systems, Remedy Software, Intuit and BigVine to illustrate the challenges and benefits of the systematic implementation of ease-of-use metrics.

Ease-of-use metrics is a simple and effective technique that has generated dozens of examples of successes, ranging from decreased customer support costs, to increased revenue, to user experience job generation during a period of layoffs. Our hope is that others will use our case studies to help demonstrate the value of user-centred design (UCD) and adopt our methods of inspiring and tracking performance.

---

1   Measures derived to assess and track usability.

THE PROBLEM: REPRESENTING THE USERS IN THE DEVELOPMENT PROCESS

You are at a company that has its own corporate culture. Your products may not be easy to use, or ease-of-use may never have been assessed. Your job is to help people with disparate attitudes and experiences to understand the value of UCD. You are also charged with changing the way employees do their jobs and with helping them to achieve success for the user and improve the bottom line. You may work with engineers who consider UCD to be largely irrelevant, designers who think that a data-driven approach to user interface (UI) design impedes creative solutions, or marketing folks who are overconfident about their ability to predict what users need. Or you may encounter all three of these kinds of people at once.

We have both worked in software development teams or at software companies that have had engineer-centric, design-centric, and/or customer-centric cultures. With no authority, no mandate, and no real credibility, we have made UCD a central part of product development and gained respect and enthusiasm for the user experience team. A key factor in our successes is the introduction and consistent tracking of ease-of-use metrics. Throughout this chapter, we will discuss what ease-of-use metrics are and how we have used them to drive success across all three cultures. But first, let's take a closer look at each of the three cultures by exploring some stereotypical employee profiles found in software companies. While stereotypes are of course unfair to some people who do not fit their confines, it is worth going over them. At the root of every stereotype is a grain of consistent truth – and these commonalities present persistent challenges that we can help you overcome.

THE ENGINEER-CENTRIC CULTURE: WE DON'T NEED ALL THAT FLUFF!

Engineer cultures are fairly easy to spot. Often they have never had a user experience group or, if they have one, the team does not have much influence on the products. Sometimes engineering teams have had a negative experience with an incompetent user experience professional – and vow to keep them at arm's length so they 'don't ruin the product again'.

As Norman (1998) points out, typical technology companies underestimate the impact and importance of user research in product development. Engineer cultures tend to focus on technology-centred, feature-driven products, to which early adopters easily adapt. The problem, of course, is that as the technology matures, the user base broadens and the user experience, rather than features alone, becomes central to the success of the product. The product team sees user experience as just another add-on.

But unless the user experience is designed around the users' needs, rather than the technology it is built upon, efforts to improve the user experience are doomed to fail. The challenge with engineer-centric cultures is communicating the users' experience of the core tasks in a language understood by people who revere logic and technology. Edward the Engineer, a composite character described below, exemplifies this particular challenge.

EDWARD THE ENGINEER

Edward is a stereotypical distinguished engineer who is somewhat socially awkward. He's excited about developing neat technology and making his mark on the product. Edward works long hours, is well respected by other engineers, thrives on thinking about 'edge' or 'corner' cases,[2] really does want to improve the user experience and believes he builds wonderful user interfaces.

Edward will invite you to his office to show you his latest accomplishments. You are expected to tell him what a wonderful job he has done. He may ask for help or advice – but will often limit your input to colours and icons. When you make substantive recommendations for changes in application flow or page layout, there often 'isn't time' or the changes are not made because they 'didn't make sense'.

When you start to press for changes, he may be insulted and become territorial – letting you know that he has done the interface for years and it works well. He may tell you that the engineers design the task flow. He may also remind you of the 'terrible things' that the last UI designer or user researcher did to the product. He will be wary of your opinion and will focus heavily on his own experience 'This is easy to do – let me show you … See, it was easy.'

CHALLENGES OF THE ENGINEER-CENTRIC CULTURE

The engineer-centric culture presents a number of challenges to user-centred design practitioners, in that engineers:

---

2   An edge case or corner case is an uncommon use case or user task, which most users would never experience. Weighing edge cases too heavily when designing an interface can make the interface significantly less usable for the majority of users.

- tend to define a product as usable if it is *possible* to do a task in the interface;

- rely heavily on their own experience;

- believe they should 'own' the product's user interface;

- feel they are doing the right thing for the customer.

THE DESIGN-CENTRIC CULTURE: BUT IT LOOKS GOOD!

Unconstrained design-centric cultures are common among Internet companies and consulting firms. Some designers view building applications and web sites as a creative endeavour that is best left to artists. While designers may believe that they know what the user experiences, their primary focus may be on creating designs that other designers will like and respect.

They may view user research as somewhat helpful, but will pick and choose what they apply to designs. When they see people having problems with their favourite designs, they may blame the user or claim that the users liked it (despite having problems). If you press them on potential solutions to problems, you may be told that you are 'doing their job' or that you are 'trying to drive the design'. Perhaps you will recognise the challenge of working with people like Dana the Designer.

DANA THE DESIGNER

Dana is somewhat introverted, buys fashionable clothes and prefers to talk about hypothetical users and creative solutions. She is suspicious of data – unless they show her designs in a positive light. She often works long hours, engages in lengthy design exercises, and believes she is methodical and builds clever UIs. If you ask to see her designs, she will comply.

During your meeting, Dana will nod and smile, but not listen carefully. Her confidence in her own design talent eclipses her interest in input from non-creative types. After usability testing, when you recommend substantive changes, there often 'isn't time' or the changes are not made because they 'don't work' with the design concept.

When you start to press for changes or ask why they 'don't work', she may become insulted and territorial. She may tell you that she has already done the designs with the user in mind and may show you her diagrams of task flows, attractive user personas or tell you about her design exercises. Her work will be very eye-catching – but because she doesn't understand the underlying customer needs, skips usability test sessions and ignores the findings, many of her designs will be difficult to use. She will be polite – but stubbornly resistant.

CHALLENGES OF THE DESIGN-CENTRIC CULTURE

The design-centric culture presents several challenges in that aesthetically-driven designers:

- define the user experience more on the basis of aesthetic experience than ease-of-use;

- often assume print visual design principles transfer directly to computer user interfaces;

- often value the user experience in terms of the visual art of a single user interface, rather than in the elegance of larger dynamic workflows;

- rely heavily on their own instincts about the users;

- attend selectively to user research, focusing only on the results that confirm their viewpoints.

THE CUSTOMER-CENTRIC CULTURE: I KNOW MY CUSTOMER!

Customer-centred cultures are often found among companies that have extensive customer outreach efforts or 'user groups' who meet and discuss issues. While this culture may seem ideal for implementing a user-centred design process, the user experience team may find unexpected resistance to their recommendations for improvement.

This is because when employees have contact with customers on a regular basis, they begin to believe that they can speak for the customer. The danger of all of these employees having experience with some customers is that they may become overconfident. People who claim to 'know the customer' are found in all professions – marketing, sales, product management, even company founders. The marketing group conducts large market research studies; product management tracks the primary complaints at the call centre and some company founders attempt to stay connected to the customer base through occasional meetings with customers.

While the insights that these groups have are all useful, the conclusions they draw may be misleading or even wrong. Take the example of Carl the Customer Advocate.

CARL THE CUSTOMER ADVOCATE

Carl speaks with 10–20 customers per year. He is extremely confident in his opinions about what customers need. However, Carl doesn't fully understand the limitations of the data he has been collecting. He may say, 'leading questions are bad' but asks them anyway. He may be able to cite some limitations of survey data, but doesn't design his survey to minimise the biases and rarely allows the flaws to temper his conclusions.

Carl will tend to listen to his 'biggest' or 'loudest' customers and generalise their needs to the needs of all users. The challenge with Carl is to make him aware of the limitations of his information. One of the most useful things a user experience professional can do for Carl is to help him understand sampling, and the fact that what users say is often different from what they actually do.

CHALLENGES OF THE CUSTOMER-CENTRIC CULTURE

Customer advocates:

- rely heavily on customers' self-report and customer suggestions to assess the usability of the interface;

- disproportionately weight their 'biggest' (that is, those with the biggest sales on the line) or 'loudest' customers;

- are often overconfident in their ability to 'know' what the customer needs;

- often believe they should 'own' the product's user interface.

THE SOLUTION: EASE-OF-USE METRICS

We have found one system that drives effective change across all these cultures. The system is to work with the entire product team to develop a common vision about ease-of-use goals and metrics and then to continually compare the current experience with those goals.

Ease-of-use metrics measure how easy or difficult a product is to use. There are many potential metrics that can be used to measure ease-of-use for a product or solution (for example, see ISO/IEC 9126-2 and ISO/IEC 9126-4, or Nielsen, 1993). These metrics fall into three main classes:

- *Effectiveness*: the ability of users to achieve specific goals;

- *Efficiency*: the resources expended in relation to the goals achieved (e.g., time to complete a task);

- *Satisfaction*: the comfort and acceptability of the interface to its users.

Generally, measures of effectiveness and efficiency are more important to product usability than measures of satisfaction. Although satisfaction questions can be derived independently, you can also use standard tests for user satisfaction (such as the SUMI, WAMMI, and SUS [3]).[4]

Although we usually employ measures of effectiveness, efficiency and satisfaction for every test, we prioritise ease-of-use based on the Ease-of-use Pyramid shown in Figure 2.1. Since measures of effectiveness, efficiency and satisfaction are not always correlated, it is important to consider which measures are most pertinent to each task or product.

As a minimum, we want to make sure that we have met our goals with respect to the effectiveness of the product. If users cannot complete a task successfully, it doesn't matter how much time they spend attempting it. We usually use task completion (the percentage of users who correctly complete the task) as the metric for our standard measure of effectiveness. For some studies, we use the average number of predefined errors[5] as an additional measure of effectiveness.

After we have met our ease-of-use goals for effectiveness, we focus on meeting our goals for efficiency. Two efficiency measures we use are time on task and task flow deviation. Time on task is the amount of time it takes, on average, to complete the task. Faster times are more desirable as long as the tasks are completed successfully. Task flow deviation is the ratio of the

---

3   See Tullis and Stetson (2004) for a comparison of surveys of web satisfaction.

4   Standard tests for user satisfaction have not been evaluated for internal consistency, test validity and reliability. Therefore, they may be 'standard', but they are not 'standardised' in the formal sense.

5   Predefined errors are errors that the team might be able to anticipate before testing. For example, pressing Cancel instead of Delete might be a predefined error for a given task in a usability test.

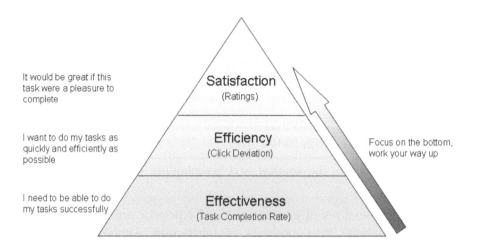

Figure 2.1   The Ease-of-Use pyramid

optimal number of steps to complete the task to the average number of steps to complete the task. The ideal value to aim for is one, where all users are using the most efficient solution to complete the task. For this measure, the fewer steps necessary to complete a task, the better.

Once users can accomplish tasks effectively and efficiently, we focus on satisfaction. Generally we employ Likert-scale ratings of satisfaction, perceived ease-of-use and confidence. However, we have found that while questionnaire data are useful, understanding *why* people rated something the way they did is usually more valuable than the rating itself. For example, someone might indicate on the questionnaire that they were not confident in whether they completed a given task correctly. But when you ask why they answered that way, you might learn that they weren't confident because the system did not provide feedback that they had done it correctly. For this reason, including cognitive interviewing techniques when participants are filling out questionnaire data is particularly useful.[6]

Figure 2.2 shows an iterative process that ultimately yields products that meet effectiveness, efficiency and satisfaction goals. For many products, simply achieving effectiveness goals (task success) may be enough.

Setting goals and tracking ease-of-use metrics is not new. A team of researchers at Bellcore in the early 1990s studied the transition of an application

---

6   See Willis (2004) for details of cognitive interviewing with questionnaires.

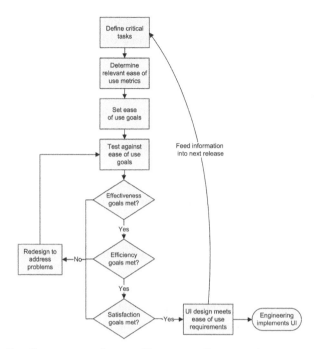

Figure 2.2   Iterative process for meeting ease-of-use goals

from a character-based to a graphical user interface (Burkhart, Hemphill and Jones, 1994). They illustrated the advantages of gathering baseline data against usability goals to determine whether a new design is better or worse than the old one.

However, very few teams appear to systematically assess their designs' performance. Indeed, the results of the 2002 survey of user-centred design practices revealed that only 14 per cent of UCD professionals use ease-of-use metrics in testing (see Vredenburg, Mao, Smith and Carey, 2002).[7]

There are many reasons that teams may not be currently using ease-of-use metrics, but one of the main reasons may be a lack of understanding of the benefits of metrics, and how metrics can be a compelling force for culture change.

THE BENEFITS OF EASE-OF-USE METRICS

Most members of product teams have the best of intentions. Edward the Engineer, Dana the Designer, Carl the Customer Advocate and other team

---

7   Only 10 per cent of UCD professionals cited users' ability to complete required tasks as a measure of UCD effectiveness.

members seek to build the features the customers want and can use. All too often, however, the final products are very difficult to use. Why does this happen? Why do good intentions fail to produce results?

Many factors affect a team's ultimate success, but usually the problem begins with subjective requirements. Requirements often state that the user interface must be 'easy to use'. Without a concrete, measurable definition, however, there is no way to determine whether the requirement has been met.

And so, opinions reign and the customer often loses. As one distinguished engineer stated while completing an arduous nine-step customer support task, 'See, this is easy to use – I did it just now.' Because this engineer was a long-time employee with good company credibility, his word carried enormous weight. If the requirement was subjective, the product would have shipped.

Fortunately, in this case the product requirement stated that '80 per cent of new users must be able to create a new customer record' and since less than 20 per cent of new users could accomplish the task, the team continued to put resources into this work and ultimately produced a more streamlined user interface that met the ease-of-use goal.

Ease-of-use metrics and ease-of-use goals provide a team with an objective measure for determining if they have or have not made a product that is 'easy to use'. Ease-of-use metrics and goals also:

- help prevent teams from getting bogged down in discussions about which employee's subjective (and often more politically powerful) opinion of user success reigns;

- motivate teams to perform at their best by giving them lucid, unambiguous goals that they can celebrate upon reaching;

- focus teams on the critical few product features;

- provide immediate feedback about which UI changes had a positive impact – and just as importantly, which ones did not;

- verify whether or not the team has met its goals;

- establish which areas of the project need more resources/attention;

- facilitate rigorous return on investment estimates.[8]

---

8   For example, correlating a UI change with a reduction in customer support calls

MOTIVATING TEAMS

Simply tracking metrics tends to boost people's performance. This phenomenon is known as the Hawthorne Effect. In 1927, researchers attempted to determine the conditions under which workers at the Hawthorne, NY Western Electric plant were most productive.

After studying multiple conditions (e.g., break schedules, lighting, bonus structures) researchers found that production increases were unrelated to the changes in working conditions. Instead, performance appeared to improve because it was being tracked overtly (for a review, see Franke and Kaul, 1978).

We see this effect today. One engineer we worked with had this to say about the ease-of-use metrics: 'Now I see why this [usability] stuff matters – and I know that I'm making a difference.'

Once metrics are being tracked, teams can further improve their performance by setting concrete, measurable goals. For more than 35 years, psychologists have studied the positive effects of goal setting. When one group of workers is given specific, concrete goals (e.g., cut down 30 logs per day) and another group is given vague goals (e.g., cut down as many logs as you can), the group with specific concrete goals performs significantly better. For example, loggers given specific goals cut down over 20 per cent more trees compared with loggers given vague goals (Latham and Kinne, 1974; Latham and Yuki, 1975). The improved performance is quite robust and has been documented across a wide variety of industries and tasks (for a review, see Locke and Latham, 2002).

By setting ease-of-use goals, UCD teams create a situation that is likely to lead to success. Ironically, we have noticed that product managers and development teams tend to set higher success goals than user researchers. A common expectation is that '100 per cent of people should be able to do all the tasks.' This may be because user researchers have a better understanding of humans, that they are imperfect systems ... or simply that they have more experience with user testing and recognise that users can often interpret interfaces in ways very different from those intended.

Either way, when most of our time is spent advocating heavily for the user (occasionally pushing the Edwards, Danas and Carls of the company to achieve higher standards), it can be refreshing to advocate easier goals. These conversations at the beginning of the project are an excellent way to develop a shared vision about the product.

Where do the concrete numbers on the ease-of-use goals come from? They can be derived from previous experience, based on rules of thumb (for example, 90 per cent of target users should be able to complete the three to five most critical tasks on most products), guided by international standards (ISO 9241-11 or ISO/IEC 9126-4), or they can be based on performance with the current method being used to accomplish the task. For example, Burkhart, Hemphill and Jones (1994) arbitrarily aimed for a goal of 50 per cent improvement over the existing method in time to accomplish a comparable set of tasks.

However, simply creating ease-of-use goals is not enough. Working across the team to ensure that everyone buys into the ease-of-use goals is critical. A few years ago we worked with one design-centric web site team that never truly bought into the importance of meeting ease-of-use goals. The team designed a solution that they liked, which was quite pretty, but when users could not buy the products they came to the site to buy, the team was reluctant to make design changes that would improve the users' performance.

This design-centric team weighted visual appeal more heavily than ease-of-use. After many millions of dollars of resources were spent, the users' ability to buy, and the revenue brought in via the web site remained *exactly the same*. In the final analysis, the ROI for that project was negative.

In contrast, a user-centred product team we worked with fully bought into ease-of-use goals and persisted on tough usability problems until they were successful. When their initial redesigns failed to meet the ease-of-use goals, the user experience team went back to the proverbial drawing board and developed several other possible interfaces.

After spending less than US$100,000 in user experience resources and US$300,000 in engineering costs, this team ultimately achieved a 95 per cent success rate on the critical tasks (an increase of over 50 per cent), which corresponded with a reduction in support calls that saved the company millions of dollars.

FOCUSING ON THE CRITICAL FEATURES

Setting concrete ease-of-use goals forces teams to think through which tasks are critical to the user – tasks most users spend most of their time doing (e.g., creating new customer records) or tasks that are essential to the user being able use the product (e.g., product installation). Typically, the experience most users have of a product is determined by a very small number of features. As Mauro (2002) found, 95 per cent of users use 5 per cent of a product most of the time and only 20 per cent of the product some of the time.

We recommend setting higher ease-of-use goals for critical tasks (e.g., 80-90 per cent of users can complete the task without help) and lower ease-of-use goals for other tasks (e.g., 60 per cent of users can complete the task without help). These ease-of-use goals clearly indicate which tasks are most important and help the team to stay focused on the core drivers of the users' experience.

PROVIDING IMMEDIATE AND OBJECTIVE FEEDBACK ON UI CHANGES

Tracking ease-of-use metrics after each iterative design change gives UCD professionals and engineers immediate, objective feedback about the effectiveness of their changes. Simply watching a usability test is not enough. We all have biases that we use to process information. For example, since we would like a redesign to be better than an existing design, we are more likely to observe problems with the existing design and dismiss minor problems that are seen with the redesign.[9] Interestingly, the more effort people put into a change, the more they need to believe that the effort was fruitful and the less likely they are to notice evidence to the contrary (see Festinger, 1957). Unfortunately, effort does not always yield results. Indeed, estimates from our experience suggest that up to 30 per cent of the time, the revised designs perform no better than (or even worse than) the original ones.

Memory also affects the conclusions people reach. Unfortunately, not all memories are equal. We typically remember more details from the first user we saw and the last user we saw than from users in the middle of a study[10]. If we do not track success rates, it is easy for teams to weight the experience of the first and last users too heavily. Not surprisingly, sessions that we observe also tend to have a greater influence on us than sessions we do not observe. Tracking success rates and other ease-of-use metrics helps to counteract these biases. By tracking ease-of-use metrics, we are able to see the bigger picture.

For example, after seeing one usability test session, an enthusiastic engineer wanted to change the flow of the application to solve the users' problem. But, after learning that only one of ten users had the problem, he agreed to solve the issues that affected more people.

By operationally defining user success at the beginning of a project and tracking user success rates across iterations, we are able to counteract many of

---

9   This is the classic 'confirmation bias' that scientists strive to avoid through use of double-blind testing. See Ditto and Lopez (1992) for further information.

10 This is the 'serial position' effect, first identified by Ebbinghaus in 1902. See also Murdock (1962) and Roediger and Crowder (1976).

our biases and make rigorously informed decisions. One user experience team we worked with attempted to make the process of printing cheques easier for new users, to compete with using financial management software. They spent more than a week developing an innovative, professional-looking design that everyone was sure would solve the problem and impress the users. Although the users said they preferred the new design, they made *just as many errors* using the new design as using the original design.

Because the new design did not meet the ease-of-use goals, the team went back to the drawing board and developed two more solutions. One solution not only met ease-of-use goals and delighted customers, but it may also be patented! Having immediate, objective feedback helped the team to determine what did and did not work and, in this case, resulted in a highly creative and successful solution. Initial estimates suggest that the cost of the solution (roughly US$50,000) is well below the expected savings (over one million dollars savings in support calls for cheque printing in the first year).

VERIFYING WHEN THE TEAM HAS MET ITS GOALS

As noted earlier, without a goal, teams cannot know whether they have achieved their objective. Just as a QA team may work with the product team to define a goal of fewer than 50 known bugs before the product is shipped, a user experience group must define the success criteria for ease-of-use. This can vary from project to project and user-group to user-group. Teams are usually very pleased to have met their ease-of-use goals – one group even gave themselves a standing ovation!

Iterative usability testing and product redesigns can have dramatic effects that are highly motivating. For example, at Intuit, after spending less than US$10,000 testing and rewriting a letter to encourage customers to update credit card information the company had on file, user success rates (and subsequent sales) increased by over 50 per cent – achieving the ease-of-use goals and increasing revenue by millions of dollars. Needless to say, the team was very satisfied with the improvements and is actively seeking additional usability resources.

Sometimes, simply showing that the team has boosted the user success rates and achieved its goals is enough for a company to fully support the User Experience team. For example, while at Peregrine Systems, Kaaren built a highly regarded group that consistently increased success rates on the critical tasks from between 0 per cent and 25 per cent to between 70 per cent and 100 per cent. While no ROI was ever calculated for these changes, the consistent production of measurable results convinced senior management that the team was a great asset to the company. Over a nine-month period in which Peregrine laid off over 50 per cent of the employees, the User Experience team increased by 20 per cent.

ESTABLISHING WHICH AREAS OF THE PRODUCT NEED MORE RESOURCES/ATTENTION

By comparing your current level of success to your goal level, your team will be able to reallocate resources more effectively. For example, in Figure 2.3 below, we see that success rates for Task 1 are 50 per cent – well below the ease-of-use goal for that task. On the other hand, success rates for Task 3 are 60 per cent – well above the ease-of-use goal. This provides clear direction for resource allocation – more time and effort need to be put into improving the interface for Task 1; little needs to be dedicated to improving the interface for Tasks 2 and 3.

Sometimes, even though user interface changes have a positive impact, the charts reveal that more work is needed. For example, at BigVine registered customers purchased an average of US$200 of merchandise each year. With the old registration process, only 18 per cent of people completed registration. After spending US$10,000 redesigning the registration process, success rates increased to 30 per cent – which translated into many thousands of dollars of additional revenue. However, despite the improvements, it was clear that further work was needed. Neither the product manager nor the company were

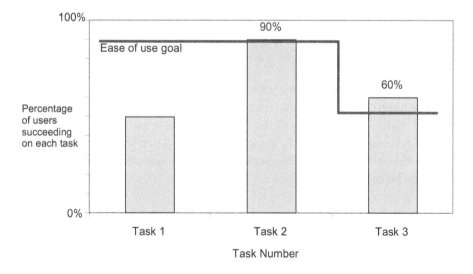

Figure 2.3   Ease-of-use goals and success rates for three tasks

satisfied with a 30 per cent completion rate. Ease-of-use metrics (in this case, success rates on the live site) established that the revised registration process, while significantly improved, required more resources.

Some companies we have worked at (Remedy, for example) have incorporated user success rates and user experience bugs (deviations between the designs and the produced product) as part of the monthly project reviews. As a result, user success rates and number of user experience bugs are two of the factors considered when deciding where to put resources and when and whether to ship a product. By having a concrete metric that could be compared with a goal, user experience became a key input into the decision-making process.

FACILITATING ROI CALCULATIONS

Tying UI changes to overall product sales, support calls or satisfaction is difficult. Most of the time, you cannot prove that an increase in revenue or a decrease in support costs is due solely to a new UI. Even if you do a usability test that shows a 56 per cent increase in effectiveness of a new user interface, you may not see a corresponding decrease in support calls. Yet, published measures of ROI make exactly those leaps.[11] The relationship between UI changes and increased revenue or decreased costs is usually correlational. When sales go up (or down), new features may have been added, the overall economy may have improved, a new advertising campaign may be particularly effective, or a competitor may have gone out of business. Similarly, the fact that there were no changes in sales does not mean that the new UI was ineffective. Only experimental designs with random assignment to condition can yield conclusions of causality.

For example, let us assume that a UCD team redesigns an e-commerce purchase path to improve the user experience. If the web site randomly assigned visitors to the old and the revised purchase paths, and three times as much revenue came from the people who went down the revised purchase path, that would be clear evidence that the UI changes affected sales and the ROI could be calculated cleanly.

In most companies, however, we rarely have the luxury of randomly assigning customers to one of two concurrently running user interfaces.

---

11   For example, Nielsen and Gilutz (2003) state 'the redesign resulted in an increase of at least 30 per cent in sales in the first quarter after the launch of the redesign' (page 31).

Instead, we work on projects where UI changes are confounded with many factors. Teasing apart the likely impact of one factor (e.g., UI changes) when multiple factors are potentially at work can be done with greater confidence by measuring the impact of our work on the user experience and then linking those measures to more messy financial ones.

The idea of measuring near-term (proximal) changes in a user interface that are not confounded with other factors and linking them to longer-term (distal) changes is found in the program evaluation literature (e.g., Weiss, 1998). In the UCD profession, proximal measures can be assessed in the lab and include standard ease-of-use metrics (i.e., task success rates, task efficiency and task satisfaction; see ISO/IEC 9126-2 and -4 for more detail). These are all measures that should be unaffected by marketing and branding and the presence or absence of a competitor. Distal measures are those that may be affected by other factors such as product revenue, number of support calls about a particular task/feature, attrition rates, and satisfaction scores. By assessing ease-of-use metrics consistently across iterations, we not only understand our impact on the user, we can also begin to make some claims about our likely ROI.

As shown in Figure 2.4, ease-of-use metrics are an important indicator of the UCD team's effectiveness.[12] If we find that 50 per cent more people can successfully file a help desk ticket, we can argue that we contributed to the decrease in support calls regarding this issue. Conversely, if we find that our user success rates have not changed, it would be difficult to claim that our new UI drove support call savings.

HOW DIFFERENT CULTURES RESPOND TO EASE-OF-USE METRICS AND GOALS

At several companies over the past ten years we have advocated setting ease-of-use goals at the beginning of the project and collecting ease-of-use metrics throughout the iterative design process. Depending on the company's culture, these efforts encounter distinct problems. What follows is a description of problems that may manifest themselves in engineer-centric, design-centric and customer-centric cultures, and of how we integrated ease-of-use metrics to improve products. Note that several cultures may be present within one company and they may well overlap.

---

12   See also HCD 3.6 (Set Quality in Use Objectives) of the Usability Maturity Model in ISO TR 18529.

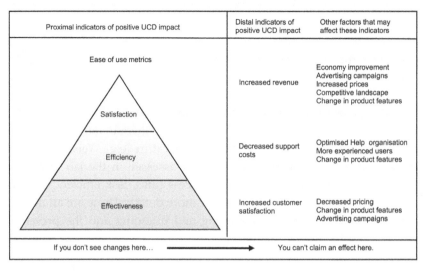

Figure 2.4   Ease-of-use metrics and indicators of UCD impact

THE ENGINEER-CENTRIC CULTURE: NUMBERS REDUCE FLUFF!

Engineer-centric cultures may equate user-centred design with unnecessary 'fluff'. Fortunately, engineers tend to respond well to data. They usually have goals for system performance, number of features implemented and number of bugs allowed. At first, the idea of setting goals for user success may seem odd, but, once explained, will be accepted quickly. When you baseline the current product, engineers may be alarmed if the success rates are low. As you progress and can demonstrate changes in user success, the charts will be interesting to the engineers – and you will develop credibility.

When you and Edward the Engineer disagree about a solution, if you suggest testing both options, he will agree. By letting the data drive the decision, Edward will learn that you too respect numbers and are not simply relying on your opinion. When Edward's solution performs better, praising his design in public – '70 per cent of users could accomplish their task with Edward's search design' – will help him to understand that you respect his abilities and are concerned about the user, not about being 'right'.

After several months, Edward will become one of your biggest champions. With time, the engineer culture will evolve into a company that systematically approaches user-centred design and tracks its effectiveness. The good news is, once you're part of the process, you'll never be forgotten.

CASE STUDY 1: EASE-OF-USE METRICS AT REMEDY

In 2000, Remedy was largely driven by its strong engineer culture. When Kaaren arrived at Remedy, only two product teams had experience with a user experience professional and one of those experiences was very negative. Many engineers had strong opinions about the user interface and insisted that it was theirs and they had done a fantastic job.

After hiring exceptional designers and user researchers, the team began to investigate Remedy's various applications. They uncovered problems, recorded current success rates, revised the user interface and demonstrated the effects of the new UI on the success rates. Some success rates immediately surpassed the goals, while others required up to three iterations before yielding major usability improvements.

By setting the standards to which the team held themselves and through constant assessment of the products, the engineers began to understand the value of user-centred design and their own opinions were stated less strongly. The originally sceptical engineers eventually became user-centred design supporters. They began suggesting that their solutions be tested, and they stopped by our offices regularly for advice.

After Wendy joined the team, they began to use user flows and screen shots as part of each Marketing Requirements Document, and the Quality Assurance (QA) team filed bugs for each discrepancy between the UI mock-ups and the product.

The Vice-President of Engineering reviewed these user experience bug rates at the bi-weekly project review meeting. Within a three-year period, all Remedy applications met or exceeded the ease-of-use goals for the critical tasks! Many of the usability improvements were upwards of 200 per cent. Most importantly, ease-of-use goals and metrics and, as a result, user-centred design, became key parts of the product development process.

THE DESIGN-CENTRIC CULTURE: BALANCING AESTHETICS WITH FUNCTIONALITY

Unrestrained design cultures will either avoid ease-of-use metrics at all costs or view ease-of-use metrics solely as a vehicle to prove what a good job they have done. In this culture, you can help designers understand the value of data by including them up front during qualitative field studies and working with them to create personas that include critical tasks and ease-of-use goals. At the same time, you will want to get product managers or business professionals to start talking about critical tasks and the performance that they expect.

With time and effort to collaborate on critical tasks and ease-of-use metrics, the designers will have a new focus on the importance of actual users completing

---

CASE STUDY 2: METRICS AT BIGVINE

BigVine, a now defunct barter web site, was founded in the dot-com heyday. The company was fast-paced and intense; a 60–80 hour work week was common and the high salaries and potential for equity attracted highly regarded professionals from all over the United States. Some attended prestigious design schools such as Parsons and business schools such as Harvard.

At first, most members of the team were wary of user research and not quite sure what usability testing would do for the company. Some found it interesting, but not related to their solution-generation techniques. After the first series of tests, one designer was quite offended that her pages were tested and did not perform well. She felt that the user research was trying to 'take over her job' and that she should be left alone to do her work as usual. A product manager also was upset that someone else had ideas for how to improve the user interface of his product.

At last, a highly competent and confident art director embraced critical user tasks and ease-of-use metrics and her work flourished. Over time, the people who addressed the key user problems had concrete evidence of their financial impact. For example, the product manager was pleased that twice as many people successfully completed a registration task (on the live site, people were randomly assigned to the old or the new registration path and the new path yielded double the number of registrants).

The user success improvements of the revised registration, product listing, and buying process, as well as estimates of the hundreds of thousands of dollars of additional revenue over time, were presented to the executive staff. Within an eight-month period, the value of user-centred design had become apparent and the unrestrained design culture began to shift to a systematic user-centred culture. One designer who valued aesthetics over functionality ultimately left the company; the remaining team easily developed a UI that met the users' needs and won multiple awards (Forbes 2000's, 'Best of the Web', Newsweek's 'Top 103 Web Sites' and Inc. magazine's 'Best Barter Site').

their tasks. Designers, and the rest of the company, will see the effectiveness of various designs and will learn what changes do and do not make a difference.

When the data show that a design made a substantial improvement, publicly spreads the word about the designers' success. By noting the progress, more people will see the relationship between addressing a user's problem and subsequent increases in success. Designers who are not particularly good at their job and those who prefer sexy designs over functional ones will eventually leave. Those who work cooperatively and design aesthetically pleasing systems that people can use will thrive. They will also appreciate knowing that their own CVs, design toolkits and marketability are being bolstered by a new understanding of user-centred design. Eventually, the company will come to accept ease-of-use metrics and rely on them as a counterweight to the myriad of opinions.

THE CUSTOMER-CENTRIC CULTURE: ESTABLISHING OBSERVATIONAL RIGOUR

Marketing researchers and product managers may think that their surveys and interviews give them all the information that they need. After all, the customer told them what they thought the big problems were. Unfortunately, customers often are not aware what is causing them difficulty, and may misattribute problem A to problem B or problem C. So customer self-reports may not uncover the true usability issues and may not be an accurate reflection of how easy the product is to use.

Similarly, user experience professionals may feel that because they do usability testing and uncover problems, formally tracking metrics is unnecessary. Unfortunately, as seen in the cheque-printing example we discussed earlier, uncovering problems (and possibly addressing them) does not guarantee that the changes lead to a more-usable design. Identifying usability problems is crucial for product development, but tracking is critical for showing change or lack thereof over time. Metrics tell you how you are doing. Identified problems tell you why.

User experience professionals also may be unsure of their effectiveness and be concerned that tracking metrics may not show them or others in a favourable light. To be fair, tracking metrics will not always show anyone in a favourable light. That is exactly the point – to learn what is working and what is not! When companies embrace the user, it is easy to get teams to address the products' shortcomings. Having them systematically assess the users' experience is more difficult, but helps everyone recognise the value of their efforts.

CASE STUDY 3: INTUIT

Intuit has always embraced the user. When he founded the company in the 1980s, Scott Cook realised that for people to use software to pay their bill and track their savings, it would need to be like entering items in the already-familiar chequebook registry – only easier. [1] *Only when this goal was achieved was Quicken released.* [2]

'Intuit's user-centred focus means that each year the company spends tens of millions of dollars to understand its customers and bring them into contact with our product development teams. However, in some cases, our efforts may be haphazard.

Like many companies, tight development deadlines mean Intuit may focus on testing new features rather than the entire product experience. As such, we may not see the big picture – or may discard the knowledge that others bring to bear. To help Intuit become more methodical, we have begun to work across the company to assess the ease-of-use of our product lines.

When the systematic collection of ease-of-use metrics was introduced, some employees didn't see the value. Some felt that that was just another layer of bureaucracy and argued that we already know what the customer wants and experiences since we talk to them. Others were reluctant to do more than find problems and allow others to solve them. There was concern that some teams may be offended that their work was being evaluated and held up against a goal.

The adoption of tracking ease-of-use metrics has benefited from Intuit's adoption of the Six Sigma Process Excellence process. [3] *With Intuit's emphasis on Six Sigma – a quality improvement methodology – we have encouraged business units to use ease-of-use metrics as one source of customer data, and to include them in their quarterly reviews.*

In this manner, all business units on a regular basis review the overall experiences our users have with the critical tasks. Fortunately, Intuit's already user-centred culture and focus on Six Sigma has made the transition to rigorous ease-of-use data collection smooth. Initial projects have led to a refocus on ensuring ease-of-use for critical tasks, and customers are hailing improvements to ease-of-use.'

---

1   Ease-of-use was assessed by measuring accuracy, time on task and satisfaction.
2   For the whole story of Quicken's success, see Taylor and Schroeder, 2003.
3   See www.sixsigma.com/sixsigma/six_sigma.asp for information about this process methodology.

SUMMARY

When user researchers rely heavily on anecdotal evidence, opinions and their ability to convince one person at a time on the product team, they are likely to fail and experience frustration – especially when they run into the Edward the Engineer, Dana the Designer and Carl the Customer Advocate. However, by methodically driving ease-of-use metrics and goals into projects, project reviews and the company culture, user experience teams are likely to succeed.

Ease-of-use metrics keep our biases in check, ensure that team successes are concrete and easy to share with others, and thus are more likely to grow organically across the company – regardless of its culture. The data-driven successes are interesting to executives, motivating to product team members and very important to the users.

The strong ties to ROI make compelling arguments about the value of user-centred design. While change is always uncomfortable for some, incorporating ease-of-use metrics will smooth your path toward transforming your company's culture and helping it to see the value of user-centred design.

REFERENCES

Bias, R.G., and Mayhew, D.J. (1994). *Cost-Justifying Usability*. San Diego: Academic Press.

Burkhart, B., Hemphill, D., and Jones, S. (1994). *The Value of a Baseline in Determining Design Success*. Proceedings of the ACM SigCHI 1994 Conference, 386-391.

Ditto, P.H., and Lopez, D.F. (1992). *Motivated Skepticism: Use of Differential Decision Criteria for Preferred and Non-preferred Conclusions*. Journal of Personality and Social Psychology, 63, 568–584.

Ebbinghaus, E. (1902). *Grundzüge der Psychologie*. Leipzig: von Veit.

Festinger, L. (1957) *A Theory of Cognitive Dissonance*. Evanston, Ill.; Row Peterson.

Franke, R.H. and Kaul, J.D. (1978). *The Hawthorne Experiments: First Statistical Interpretation*. American Sociological Review, 43, 623–643.

ISO (2003). ISO/IEC TR 9126-2:2003. *Software engineering – Product quality– Part 2: External metrics.* www.iso.org/iso/en/CatalogueDetailPage.CatalogueDetail?CSNUMBER=22750&scopelis

ISO (2004). ISO/IEC TR 9126-4:2004. *Software engineering – Product quality – Part 4: Quality in use metrics.* www.iso.org/iso/en/CatalogueDetailPage.CatalogueDetail?CSNUMBER=39752

Latham, G.P. and Kinne, S.B. (1974). *Improving Job Performance Through Training in Goal Setting.* Journal of Applied Psychology, 59, 187–191.

Latham and Yuki, G.A. (1975). *Assigned Versus Participative Goal Setting with Educated and Uneducated Wood Workers.* Journal of Applied Psychology. 60, 299–302.

Locke, E.A., and Latham, G.P. (2002) *Building A Practically Useful Theory of Goal Setting and Task Motivation.* American Psychologist, 57, 705–717.

Mauro, C.L., (2002). *Professional Usability Testing and Return on Investment as It Applies to User Interface Design for Web-Based Products and Services.* Mauro NewMedia Inc. www.taskz.com/pdf/MNMwhitepaper.pdf

Murdock, B.B., Jr. (1962). *The Serial Position Effect of Free Recall.* Journal of Experimental Psychology, 64, 482–488.

Nielsen, J. (1993). *Usability Engineering.* San Diego, CA: Academic Press.

Nielsen, J., and Gilutz, S. (2003). *Usability Return on Investment.* Neilsen Norman Group. www.nngroup.com/reports/roi

Norman, D.A. (1998). *The Invisible Computer: Why Good Products Can Fail, The Personal Computer Is So Complex, And Information Appliances Are The Solution.* Cambridge, MA: The MIT Press.

Pressman, R. S. (1992). *Software Engineering: A Practitioner's Approach.* New York: McGraw Hill.

Roediger III, H.R., and Crowder, R.G. (1976). *A Serial Position Effect in Recall of United States Presidents.* Bulletin of the Psychonomic Society, 8, 275–278.

Taylor, S. and Schroeder, K. (2003). *Inside Intuit: How the Makers of Quicken Beat*

Microsoft and Revolutionised an Entire Industry. Boston: Harvard Business School Press.

Tullis, T.S., and Stetson, J.N. (2004). *A Comparison of Questionnaires for Assessing Web site Usability.* Presented at the UPA 2004 Annual Conference.

Vredenburg, K., Mao, J., Smith, P., and Carey, T. (2002). *A Survey of User-Centered Design Practice.* Proceedings of CHI 2002, 4, 471–478. Available at www. jeffmcneill.com/service/www/userCenteredDesignPractice.pdf

Weiss, C. (1998). *Evaluation Methods for Studying Programs And Policies.* New York: Prentice Hall.

Willis, G.B. (2004). *Cognitive Interviewing: A Tool for Improving Questionnaire Design.* London: Sage Publications.

CHAPTER 3

Tales from the Trenches: Getting Usability Through Corporate

Francis (Hank) Henry

GESTATING USABILITY

In 2001 JCPenney launched a brand new web site. This wasn't a case of gradual evolution or iterative change, nor was it just a case of 'perfuming the pig'. This was an all-out, 100 per cent code-rewrite, dynamite and rebuild extravaganza, featuring external contractors writing 'mystery code' (so nicknamed because no one inside the company really knew how to modify or maintain it), and new concepts for classifying and presenting products.

This type of 'punctuated evolution' on a major web site seems to be rare today – and is very scary to undertake. Indeed, Jared Spool (2003) has written about what he calls the 'quiet death of the major re-launch'. Nowadays caution rules, and budgets are only now reaching the levels of the bubble-era Wild Wacky Web.

Had they to do it over again, I doubt that JCPenney would contemplate such a radical redesign. But back in the age of Internet pure plays, the old-line bricks-and-mortar businesses were feeling the heat. They had to do SOMETHING, for gosh sake, to remain relevant and competitive or these splashy upstarts would eat their lunch! The scenario had changed! Their paradigm had shifted!

It was into this heady, sweaty environment that I stepped in April of 2000. But how did I, a fellow with dual degrees in Chemistry and Theatre, come to be associated with the (very successful, by the way) jcpenney.com? And wherefore … usability?

I had been with Penney at that point for about 12 years in a number of various guises, first as a member of the women's apparel group and then in an operations and communications role in product and brand development. While in that job I had the pleasure of becoming involved with the vendor selection process for arizonajeans.com, a marketing-oriented web site whose purpose was to try to keep the Arizona brand top-of-mind for teens. This web site (which is no more; Arizona branding is now part of the overall jcpenney.com site, albeit without the fun interactive items) involved gaming, music, celebrity spotting and extreme sports – the usual mélange of 'stuff' that marketers thought would attract teens to the web site. It was here that I was first exposed to a web site-building strategy, and also here where I began to understand how 'corporate' thinking could either help or hinder a web effort.

Arizonajeans.com was the brainchild of the Arizona corporate brand manager. Was he a pierced, bleached, goateed webbie who spent quality time at the football table? Far from it. He was a gruff, chain-smoking ex-denim buyer who had the term 'baleful stare' down to a fine art. He was also one of the most respected people in the denim business, and one of the finest students of his business and his customer that I ever had the pleasure to know. He possessed one characteristic that I tried to emulate all the rest of my Penney career: a passion for his business, and a passion for his customer. Let's call him Ed.

Ed had a tough time selling arizonajeans.com, even though the investment to develop it would be relatively small. He kept running into the same question: 'What's the sales plan?'

'There isn't one', Ed would growl. 'That's not the POINT! We want the site to build the brand, not try to sell the product! That can happen through the other channels!'

Often a blank stare would greet this statement. It was an early clue to me that there might be some managers – well-meaning, competent managers in their niche, be it cataloguing or bricks-and-mortar retailing, who thought that the web should just represent a carbon copy of those efforts. Personally I rejected this thesis: like Ed, I was convinced that the channels should indeed complement, support and leverage each other's strengths as well as asset expenditure ... but that selling on the Web was different and needed to be treated as such. But that's fodder for another chapter.

My role in the development of arizonajeans.com was simply to monitor the budgets, help with the selection of the vendor and to do whatever I could to promote its existence throughout the entire JCPenney community. Looking back, the competitive presentations from the potential vendors excited me about the power of this new medium. The site ended up getting a LOT of traffic. Auto manufacturers actually gave us vehicles to give away as sweepstake prizes, because the number of 'hits' was so compelling – even though in those days nobody actually had a firm definition of what a hit represented.

I went over to the Internet group in April of 2000. This team had been housed 15 miles down the road from the corporate mother ship, in the Dallas data centre with the IT group – a masterstroke, in my opinion, of organisational prescience. One must remember that in those pre-dot-bomb days, the Internet held a certain mystique. Ordinary corporate managers didn't quite understand it, and indeed many feared it. Internet sales volumes were at the time the proverbial wart on an elephant's behind, and so most of the normal management attention getters (Is this big enough to pay attention to? Will it affect my bonus?) did not apply.

Most managers were happy to delegate the Internet thing off to somebody else while they concentrated on the Really Important Matters. To JCPenney's credit, they had a few visionary managers not only in the Internet group, but also in the catalogue group of which the Internet initiative was a part. The former CEO also bought into the potential and devoted a considerable chunk of IT budget to the development of an Internet structure … at the expense of the paper catalogue.

This was a two-edged sword: it allowed jcpenney.com to develop a platform of content management, e-publishing capability and user interface that continues to be a competitive edge. The downside was that this platform was grafted onto an existing paper catalogue fulfilment infrastructure whose base code contains lines that were chiselled into rock on the walls of caves. While hopefully seamless to the customer, the back-end stuff to this day presents challenges that keep the operations folks jumping through hoops.

After several years of having a dog's breakfast of a site, JCPenney was in the throes of preparing to 'architect' an 'experience': that is, a site which it was hoped would be compelling and inviting to its target customer rather than a soulless order-taking environment with no really coordinated look and feel. At that time the home page was replete with a 'logo farm': a section right below the fold with blinky-linkies to offers as diverse (and fragmented) as Omaha steaks and Wisk detergent. Left-hand navigation consisted of fly-out menus that not only frustrated the visually and mechanically less-than-adept, but acted differently on different browsers. If you were a Mac user, you were relegated to a completely different site with text links. It was time for a change.

My job when I arrived was to act as a coordinator/translator/wheedler. The outside consultant wasn't talking to the creative community. IT wasn't talking to the merchants. And nobody was talking to marketing. I acted as a kind of shuttlecock, bouncing between the groups, enunciating deadlines, asking for favours and pointing out issues. It was a heady time and a fantastic opportunity to learn a lot in a small amount of time.

Naturally there were problems. 'What do you mean, the new navigation only supports three clicks? I have six levels of fly-out now!'; 'What do you mean, I have to provide filters by price?'; 'What do you mean, we can't support this promotion because we can't have a per cent off and a price break at the same time?'

One by one, we grabbed these issues and overcame them. And finally, on February 13th, 2001 (post-Christmas, unfortunately, but the site was NOT ready for prime time in December) we gave birth to jcpenney.com, version 5.0. Huzzahs sounded throughout the land – or at least in North Dallas.

Almost immediately after launch, the chief contractor for the rebuild, whose developers wrote all the code and designed all the templates, imploded. Went belly-up. Ceased to be. Shuffled off this virtual coil. Dot-bombed.

The contractor had crafted many functions of the site. This included site search, which had been welded together by the contractor working with the search engine vendor. Unfortunately for us, we were able to carry out very little knowledge transfer to IT before the e-bituary was penned. This meant that our IT staff had little exposure to its inner workings and almost no inkling of how the engine itself actually processed queries. Search quickly became a back-burner function and was allowed to run itself, as the inevitable post-launch 'uh-ohs' manifested themselves and consumed our time.

It was around this time that the Vice President of Infrastructure and Technology, a real visionary, decided to try something new. Up until then, the contractor had handled usability testing – or any type of usability evaluation at all. It was all summative testing, coming at the 'end', costing big bucks and revealing issues that nobody could address … the usual scenario. IT didn't quite know what usability was and often confused it with QA evaluation and user-acceptance testing. Deadlines ruled the day.

The vice president's idea was to create a new position whose job it would be to get to understand the customer. Go shopping with her (jcpenney.com's customers are almost two-thirds 'her'). Watch her shop, both physically and virtually. Understand what parts of the experience frustrated, and what parts satisfied. Get inside her head and try to see where a site like jcpenney.com could solve a problem, answer a question, replace a time-consuming or cumbersome process in her busy, time-starved, overloaded life. This position would then recommend strategic and tactical directions that could be taken to the marketers, the merchants and/or the technicians to help align the capabilities of the site to the goals of the consumer.

So a (slightly) overweight middle-aged Irishman from South Jersey becomes the Customer Experience Manager for one of the most successful e-commerce sites in the nation. I was offered this position not because of my massive human–computer interaction qualifications, but because I seemed to have some credibility and ability to work well politically with all of the groups involved. After all, I had got through the launch without getting fragged. People liked me, seemed to respect me, and were willing to give me a hearing … at least once.

Best of all, we got lucky and were able to hire a very talented usability architect (I'll call her Becky), who had been working in the web space since 1994. She had been a creative director at a web development firm as well as an account representative, information architect and general all-around web-oriented Type A. She was one of the people who worked on the very first EDS web site. In short, she 'had chops'. She joined us in January 2001, and very shortly thereafter the firm she had been with cratered. I learned a great deal from her over the three years we worked together.

So there we were: two people staring into the abyss, whose job it was to make the site better. We had no power and no staff, but boy, did we have chutzpah!

Our very first usability testing activities started off with a few outsourced tests, using a well-known usability firm based in Dallas. We did identical controlled scenarios on both the old and the new web sites, to see if we could document any noticeable improvements in time on task or ease of navigation. I remember that what I saw during those first rounds knocked my socks off.

I had no idea. I was dumbfounded, flabbergasted. Those customers did so many things, went down so many paths, performed so many loop-the-loops and barrel rolls that I would never have dreamed of doing, that I was reduced to a wheezing, reeling, glassy-eyed lunatic. This was my first mind-numbing, eye-opening exposure to the power of usability testing. I began to glimpse the value of 'test early, test often'. I was so juiced up by the experience that I fired off an email to the entire organisation detailing what I felt to be the 'low-hanging fruit' revealed by the test. I just wanted to share these remarkable insights!

Later, I was admonished for doing this and told to consider how to 'formalise' my presentation of these data. If you are starting off a usability effort, be ready for this: sometimes managers will be unwilling to socialise the results of testing without filtering them politically. This is often self-serving, but in the case of your usability management champion consider it wise. Listen to their reasoning and heed it. Voice your disagreements and hash it out.

After all, if this person has demonstrated their belief in the power of usability, they must already have a feel for how it will be greeted within the organisation. Learn from them. Why? Because I cannot think of a usability practitioner I have ever met who had the authority, on their own say-so, to force change. Lots of responsibility, yes, but little authority. Most of us need allies and also need a little bit of marketing.

It was only after several rounds of observation and lots of seminars and book learning, I felt that, maybe, we could envision a day when we might take testing activities in-house. More on that later.

As a newly minted 'Customer Experience Manager', I educated myself as best I could in usability best practices and practical usability. I attended seminars and took tutorials. I read and sat before Nielsen, Spool, Molich, Norman, Krug and many other heavyweights. I worked with local usability labs to understand their methodologies. I participated as a test subject. I attended UPA and ACM SIGCHI conferences. I attended IBM's 'Make IT Easy' programmes and learned the principles of User-Centred Design. I attended several other user-design and usability engineering training courses. Finally, 'Becky' and I both went back to graduate school, with me pursuing an MBA in e-Business and she pursuing her Master's in Cognitive Science.

In short, we tried to learn as much as we possibly could so that our recommendations would be coming from an informed background, and so we could take ourselves as far away from our own personal biases and opinions as possible. JCPenney, although they do not offer tuition reimbursement, supported us by allowing us to buy the literature and attend some of the conferences and seminars. But we still had to get creative to get resources.

As I said, we had nothing. No recruiting. No budget for incentives. No staff other than Becky and myself, with no administrative help. How could we get started?

As the senior person who knew people, I leveraged relationships. I called in favours. I begged. I tried as best I could to charm. We performed a feat known in Penney parlance as 'extending our staffs'.

What this means is that we got folks from other areas to work for us for free. I approached the folks who ran the JCPenney television studios (once used for daily HQ-to-store broadcasts, and actually quite state of the art) to see if there was any way I could use the facilities as a lab to record usability tests. Not only did those very supportive people agree to let me use the lab during down periods, but they also gave me the services of a producer! All it cost my area was the price of tape stock.

We set up a card table in front of the cafeteria, put a sign on an easel and popped a tape of a testing session into a monitor, and recruited users from the JCPenney general population. As long as their managers approved, we'd ask for an hour of their time down in the studio to help us test the new site, paper prototypes, competition, or whatever else was on our agenda for that day. I was pleased to discover that once they got into the studio and got through the briefing, they lost themselves in the tasks at hand and were able to make the rather intimidating soundstage environment 'go away'.

A word about this methodology. Was it ideal? No way. Did these employees mirror the target customer? Generally yes, but they knew a little too much. Terminology. Nomenclature. Even navigation could be affected, since try as we might, it's often difficult to completely divorce company organisation from a company's web site and navigation structure. We used these employees because they were free, available and willing, but we had to bear in mind that there were some tests whose results would be affected – even polluted – because of the very fact that they had been so deeply exposed to the Penney shtick.

Another danger of this approach is that it can cost you some credibility. While the tests provided a lot of fresh, actionable insights, there were those who didn't buy into the results simply because employees were used (particularly when the findings didn't jibe with their opinions). Finally, recruiting is hard! It takes a lot of time and follow-up, and we ended up with our original list of 150 volunteers dwindling down to about 25 or 30. We were forced to use them several times each, and they became 'expert testers'. That's a bad deal.

But, one must remember that nothing ventured, nothing gained. If we didn't use our 'extended staff' at all, we'd learn nothing. And we learned plenty; we simply had to be careful to consider the users' backgrounds and possible biases when interpreting the results.

Eventually, out of sheer frustration at the time we were wasting on recruiting and the danger of losing some credibility, we wrote a formal proposal to hand over recruitment to an outside source. The proposal was blessed. We were then able to write targeted screeners for recruitment, assign the job to a market research firm, and get that monkey off our backs.

In my opinion, this led to much richer results in the lab. It was like switching from black and white to colour. We used JCPenney gift cards as incentives, which was politically easy to sell and allowed us to avoid handling cash, which would have been a concern to me as well as being 'auditor-bait'. This practice may or may not have acted as a filter up front, limiting our participants to those willing to shop at Penney – but in Dallas, Penney is somewhat ubiquitous and we seemed to attract both Penney and non-Penney shoppers with this incentive structure. Unfortunately, due to time pressures and budgets we never got to take our act on the road. We would have loved to do some in-home testing. Or even in-office testing. ('Fess up, now, you've shopped online at work, haven't you?')

In addition to using the JCPenney television studios as a lab, we built a 'guerrilla' lab in our own offices for a few thousand dollars. This was not just Nielsen's discount usability testing, it was fire-sale usability testing. However, un-pretty as it was, it got the job done, and allowed us to tape sessions with picture-in-picture. We were also able to project the sessions into an adjacent conference room for observers.

The point is: do not hold out for a lovely lab with a one-way mirror and the latest equipment. If you can talk your company into this, fine. Much of it can also be rented if you are on a temporary gig. But you don't really need it. Usability testing can be done with a notepad and pencil – and indeed, must be if you are doing field studies. Let me explain why.

If you haul a camera and microphone into a person's workspace, you will not only succeed in making them uncomfortable, you'll also attract lots of unwanted attention from co-workers. So don't!

It's kind of like the 'observer effect': the very act of observing an event changes the event. There are many great treatises on how to conduct field studies, and I don't propose to discuss them here. Just Do It, and get what you can get. The context of the work (or home) environment is very rich. You will be hamstrung a bit by the fact that your notes will be your only guides, but even in lab-based testing where video is involved I've rarely seen anyone go back to it. Notes rule, so make sure yours are as complete as you can make them in real time. However, in a lab environment, you cannot take notes yourself if you are actively facilitating the test.

Trust me on this: if you are the one sitting with the user, doing the 'active listening' as well as the warm-up and the post-test debriefing, you will not have the cognitive capacity to remember everything you've observed. You need somebody else, if only to argue that what you saw was also what they saw. You will be somewhat tired by the third user and thoroughly burned out by the sixth. You need another viewpoint. It's hard work to facilitate a test, and you usually will not have the time (or desire) to review all the tapes once the test is over. A second pair of eyes is invaluable.

So there we were: a cheap lab in place, enough methodology to run some pretty effective testing, but still we lacked resources. For one thing, we had no designer assigned to us, nor any coders who could whip up lo-fi prototypes. We never got over that bugaboo, and so had to beg resources wherever we could.

This is where the philosophy of 'nothing succeeds like success' comes into play. Once we had a very well-received project under our belts (a rewrite of the checkout process), our credibility grew and we were able to ask folks from all areas to do things for us … off the books. They agreed because they wanted to; they considered it progressive and creative; and they had seen the results and been persuaded by members of their own cohort groups that, maybe, our contribution just might have value.

So as a result, we had designers who were dying to break out of their workaday world (how many banners for placement on MSN can you craft?) and coders who, whenever they could, would help us because they had been exposed to our methodology, seen its value, and wanted to help the customer!

To me, this is nirvana. When all members of your team understand customer's and their needs and can argue on their behalf in a meeting, you have found the common ground that the philosophy of UCD and 'interdisciplinary teamwork' refers to and seldom achieves.

BESMIRCH THE SEARCH

I would like to offer a story on one particular project that we tackled because I believe that it will eventually have as much impact on sales and profits at jcpenney.com as anything else we did.

When the new Customer Experience group was created (population: two), there was no clear understanding of exactly what the workload would be. As a result, the group was also given the responsibility of managing site search. Recall that the search experience had been crafted by the now-defunct chief contractor for the site relaunch, and it had been wheezing along on life support ever since. There had been no knowledge transfer to our IT group, and the attitude had been 'set it and forget it'.

When we inherited search it was pretty much in shambles. The IT group had not developed a positive relationship with the search vendor, and indeed communication between JCPenney and the vendor was almost non-existent. My boss proposed that I take hold of this relationship and repair it. I did this as best I could, and eventually repaired the relationship into a true partnership that yielded benefits for both parties. The vendor actually even gave me the temporary use of server licences (normally costing tens of thousands of dollars each) for free so that I could get through the holiday season when we discovered we might have capacity issues. Now that's a partner!

At this point the search experience was, to be charitable, the pits. There was no maintenance of the synonym files. There was no way out if the user hit a 'null' result. And when they did, they were slapped with an unfriendly, accusatory error message for their troubles. The search results consisted of a list of long text links based upon the navigation stream with no visual cueing of product. It was sorted on a relevance algorithm, so that if a user typed in a phrase that crossed departments (for instance, 'pants') the list of links had no apparent organisation by department, as illustrated by Figure 3.1. The number of pages of link results had no cap. And on and on.

We went to work and begged for a report that would allow us to at least view the logs of terms input by the customer into the search engine. After many weeks, we got the first report: a single day in August that contained over 23,000 unique search terms. It yielded so many golden nuggets that we lusted for more. As time progressed, our intrepid IT partners rolled up their sleeves and produced a suite of applications for us that allowed us not only to parse these logs, but also to combine time periods and sort the data.

```
                    Search results for: jacket

            We found matching items for "jacket" in the following areas.
            Please click on one of the categories below to see these products.

                          Categories 21 - 40 of 100

              [ << Previous 20 Categories ]  [ Next 20 Categories >> ]

   Confidence        Category

     100%        men's : shop by brand : jeep : outerwear                         view
     100%        women's : business casual : jackets                              view
     100%        women's : weekend wear : jackets                                 view
     100%        men's : outdoors : jackets                                       view
     100%        men's : traditions shop : outerwear                              view
     100%        women's : maternity special size li : sweaters&jackets           view
     100%        men's : shop by brand : excelled leathers : jackets-coats        view
     100%        women's : shop by size : plus sizes : tops & jackets : blazers&jackets view
     100%        women's : shop by brand : sag harbor : jackets                   view
     100%        women's : must haves : jackets                                   view
     100%        men's : summer fun shop : jackets                                view
      99%        women's : maternity photo promotion                             view
      99%        women's : maternity : denim                                     view
      99%        women's : tops & jackets : blazers & jackets                    view
      99%        online outlet store : women's : activewear                      view
      99%        women's : pants & denim : denim shop                            view
      99%        women's : shop by size : tall sizes : sale                      view
      99%        women's : showing in style : career                            view
      99%        women's : showing in style : weekend                           view
```

Figure 3.1   Example search results page from jcpenney.com prior to redesign

The *pièce de résistance,* however, was an application that allowed us (non-coders) not only to manipulate the synonym files, but also to add links to non-merchandise results. Thus, if the search engine returned no results for 'couch' because we called it 'sofa' on the site, we were able to allow the engine to equate the two terms. If a person put the term 'jobs' or 'credit' or 'annual report' into the engine (which happened thousands of times every week) we could give them a link to the appropriate content instead of a dead end. All on the fly, every day, without IT having to create XML files or touch any code. I must say, this was incredibly powerful and I tip my hat to them. Once we had these tools in place we started a division-wide programme we called 'Besmirch the Search', wherein we asked all jcpenney.com employees to be on the lookout for and to report weird or unsatisfactory search behaviour. In most cases we had a fix up the next day.

Our real first clue that our search needed some help was in the lab. Whenever we could, we would ask our testers to go shopping for an item (a pair of jeans for your daughter) and watch what happened without leading them down one road or another. Sometimes they searched, and this is where we started to notice things.

Once they entered their search query and hit 'Go', we noted some interesting behaviour. Pursed lips. Furrowed brows. A quick pull of the head backwards, away from the screen, as if something offensive was stuck to it. When we politely asked, 'Is this what you expected to see?' the response was almost invariably 'No! Where's the products?' The participants would then laboriously begin to read the lists of blue links they were confronted with.

Very, very few customers ever went to the second page of links, and nobody went to the third unless they were, frankly, computer geeks. When confronted with a dead-end null result, frustration would build and abandonment became a risk. And the ultimate sin was when multiple links all led to the exact same product, and the customer would 'pogo stick' (thanks, Jared Spool) from the search results back to the list multiple times. My favourite all-time example of this was when, while shopping for a gift for her husband, a woman searched on the term 'battery charger'. There was exactly one battery charger on the site, but because it had been categorised in multiple places, eight (!) different links all led to the same one. When she encountered this and began to pogo stick back and forth, you could almost see the smoke coming out of her ears. She did not hesitate to voice her displeasure. Quite vehemently, in fact.

Only about one-third of the people who used search knew what the 'confidence' ranking meant. Most users literally blanked it out, kind of like 'banner blindness'. If it made no sense to them, they tuned it out. Yet another little negative experience.

Once we had seen these types of scenarios repeated over and over again, we began to get a dim clue that, maybe, our search wasn't all it was cracked up to be. An extensive review of competitors' sites revealed that jcpenney.com was virtually alone in not offering product thumbnails in the initial search results screen, even if it was there to simply act as a signpost.

Eventually, through a series of lab-based observations and focus groups, we were able to crystallise our thoughts into a plan of action to make search better. We developed a short list of objectives and hypotheses that guided our thinking, which included the following:

• Don't mess with 'advanced search' up front.

- All the customer wants is a box and a go button.

- Too many drop-downs, text fields, and radio buttons will only be off-putting.

- Give the customer visual cueing (product) on the initial results page, even if it's only to support the 'scent of navigation'.

- If the customer needs to filter or sort, gently put the tool in their hands only at the point where they need it.

- If a search term is too broad (like 'pants'), provide a clear, visually cued pathway that emulates the customer's department store shopping paradigm (men's, women's, children's).

- If a search yields no results, the search engine should make intelligent suggestions as to what the customer might be looking for, or at least offer another search box as an escape hatch. No dead ends!

- Get to product thumbnail gallery as soon as the number of unique products allows. If there's only one product, take the customer there immediately.

This seemingly simple list of requirements really illustrates the Texas phrase 'says easy, does hard'. But now we felt that we had a pretty good sense of what search should do.

Now is when the corporate story gets interesting. We first pitched a search redesign to our boss, who empathised with our viewpoint but was a bit surprised at our vehemence. After all, had our customer-care representatives been fielding numerous complaints about search? No, but, we argued, customers had low expectations for search anyway, and we were consistently meeting those low expectations. And then, if people have yet another lousy search experience, are they going to pick up the phone and yell, like they might with a lousy fulfilment experience? Probably not – they'd just take it over to Lands End or Target, and we'd be none the wiser.

Wouldn't a better search experience, we argued, be a great way to engender that level of 'surprise and delight' that we were striving to achieve on our site? Wouldn't it be great if searches performed on jcpenney.com (millions and millions; one of the most-overlooked primary navigation vehicles on the site) got a pleased 'Oh!' from the customer rather than pursed lips and a furrowed brow?

The boss 'got it'. He listened, reviewed our results, and took it to his superiors: the ones who ultimately would need to approve the funding and IT resources to allow us to embark upon our vision. He was a little bit wide-eyed when he came back.

'They don't think there's anything wrong with search', he told us as we convened to hear what happened. 'They think search is just fine the way it is.'

We were stunned. We looked at each other, and then back at our VP. 'Yeah,' I ventured, 'but they're middle-aged male Penney technophiles who have used the search a million times (I was describing myself, I realised with a start). 'What about "her"? She's a lot different from them.'

The boss concurred. Over the next several months, we spent a lot of time building our case, documenting our experiences, and creating PowerPoint decks. This was one of the few occasions where I have actually gone into the video archives and pulled out tapes to make highlight clips. The upshot: the project got funding, the momentum swelled behind it, and as of this writing the new search experience is due to launch in a couple of weeks. Even though I'm not still with JCPenney, I hope you'll like it. I hope you may even say 'Oh!' Please, I beg you, don't furrow your brow.

This is but one of many projects that followed a similar trajectory: the customer surfaced the issue. Subsequent interfacing with the customer confirmed the issue was real and suggested ways to improve the experience. The argument was prepared and presented with all appropriate genuflecting to the High Court. The end result rode entirely upon the credibility of our findings, and very much upon our credibility as individuals.

GETTING THE USER (CUSTOMER) IN FRONT

In conclusion, I'd like to offer a number of broad observations about trying to get something called 'usability' or 'customer focus' infected like a virus throughout a large organisation. Some of these observations have been codified in such excellent works as Eric Schaeffer's 'Institutionalization of Usability' (2004) so I won't rehash them; I'll merely try to point out what I experienced and let you decide what's valid for your circumstance.

IT'S ALL ABOUT YOU, KID

Your personal credibility, your ability to communicate with disparate groups, your ability to stay on message, and your ability to know when you don't know doodley-squat are key. I cannot overstate the importance of the personal credibility of any usability practitioner in a corporate environment. The only power you have is how convincing your evidence is and how compellingly you can make your case. To this end, your methodologies must be sound and your impartiality above reproach. Your ability to clearly state the issues for the user in an unbiased, factually well-constructed way is critical.

Since you have no power, the entire concept of usability needs to be supported by somebody who does. You have no doubt heard about the need for a 'management champion'. It is absolutely true. The higher up the better. I was once given the opportunity to have the CEO of a US$30 billion company attend a usability session. I was then asked by lower-level management not to do so, since they felt that the exposure of a 'usability' effort to such a high level of management might be politically dangerous. In hindsight I should have jumped all over it, and used the old 'ask for forgiveness rather than permission' gambit. This CEO would have been enthralled. The point is, you need a high-level champion. Get one. Or ten.

Not everybody knows about usability and user-centred design approaches like you do. You will need to be a source of education. Even the best marketers, merchants or IT people need to be educated to the value of the process, and understand that it's not 'just testing'. Understand their concerns.

IT is driven by schedules, deadlines, and asset availability. They will react negatively to anything that they think will add time to the process. Understand, sympathetically, that they may confuse iterative usability testing with 'QA testing' or 'acceptance' testing, which comes at the end. Your job is to show them that this mysterious process called 'usability' actually reduces the need for rewrites by delivering a superior project the first time.

You can do this by choosing a project that you know you can handle, and by making the IT representatives a complete partner in your interdisciplinary project team. IT people will absolutely become enthralled when exposed to the user. Make sure they're there, and make sure their thoughts are sought out as to solutions to the dilemma at hand as your iterative process unfolds. Develop personas to communicate with the team if you need to. After a while, your relationship with the IT team will become optimised, as they come to realise the quality of the product your team has produced. Praise their contribution lavishly. It couldn't happen without them.

Marketers occupy one of the most precarious positions in any organisation. Any sales downturn is promptly blamed on marketing. Their entire focus is on achieving the sales plan. They are generally isolated and often unloved. Unless you are reporting to the marketing organisation (and I hope you aren't, because of the inherent conflict of interest between the user and the marketer), cracking that silo may be difficult.

Marketers know a lot. They invariably know about marketing on the Internet. What they may not be able to fully appreciate, except in the abstract, is that people generally resent being marketed to ... especially out of context, as they are attempting to complete an online task.

My favourite story is about a plan to offer (via an intrusive pop-up, no less) magazine subscriptions right smack in the middle of the checkout process. On jcpenney.com, mind you, which is surely everybody's destination for magazines. Isn't it yours?

YOU WILL NOT WIN ALL THE TIME

There will be times when the wishes of the user or customer will have to be subservient to the needs (or politics) of the business. Face it, if we were able to accommodate everything the customer wanted, shipping would always be free and everything would be on sale or clearance.

For instance, home page turf battles will rage, and home page real estate will be controlled by the most politically powerful – even if it means the home page looks like a dog's breakfast. Many folks will want 'their' realm showcased on the home page, relevance to the advancement of the overall business notwithstanding. Many merchants will want 'their' key item on the home page, all the time.

Your best bet here is to tread lightly, and try to emphasise quietly what a home page is for: to provide the branding cues, set the expectations for the customers, and to get them to engage with the site. Let your management champion spearhead the home page battles. Point out the opportunities, but let your management champion do the fighting.

PICK YOUR BATTLES

Not everything is worth going to the mat for. Be sure that the issues that are really critical are properly prioritised as such, and that the issues that are not do not consume the same resource allocation. I have seen some usability people alienate themselves by 'majoring in the minors' and crowing about every little issue.

BE SENSITIVE

Be aware that folks may be upset by what they observe or what you report. It's the 'Lady, your baby is ugly' syndrome. People who work so hard to make the site work can be understandably upset or offended if you use your report to attack or belittle the site.

So, be careful how you deliver your message. Present your case, but do it in a positive, respectful, collaborative spirit. Point out the good stuff, compliment the group, and then introduce the negative stuff in a way that allows positive interaction. Always praise what's working and deliver your findings in the spirit of 'what the customer seems to be telling us' and what we can all do to make it even better.

TEST EARLY AND OFTEN

Do not be inhibited from testing because you don't have a room with one-way glass or because the newest version is not online yet or you can't find the perfect target user. As we have described above, you can test and get meaningful results at any stage of the process ... even with hand-drawn representations on index cards of what your prospective page might do.

GET OUTSIDE THE WALLS WHEN RECRUITING TEST PARTICIPANTS

A lot of organisations simply grab a few co-workers for testing. While this can sometimes lead to useful results, it is always best to get folks who are not familiar with your jargon or your organisation structure (which inevitably creeps into the navigation scheme and compartmentalisation of a site).

There are plenty of market research firms who can do the recruiting for you. Look in the Yellow Pages or search on 'market research firms' on the web. It cost me US$80 per user in Dallas, and we used US$50 in JCPenney gift cards as incentive. (You may wish to use a more-generic incentive, like cash or merchandise.) These costs will vary from city to city, but even getting a few users from outside will add richness to your results. Not only that, but it gets the recruiting monkey off your back.

DON'T BECOME A VIDEO EDITOR

Yes, it's great to have a record of your test sessions, and it's a powerfully persuasive tool if you incorporate video clips into your results presentation. But please believe me: most of the video you produce will remain in the closet, unwatched, until the shelves buckle. Believe me also when I tell you that editing video is a major pain, particularly if you are working with analogue media such as videotape.

If you've gone digital, terrific, but video editing is still startlingly time-consuming. Use it if appropriate, but remember that you are not producing timeless drama for the ages; you are merely documenting a test. Don't get all caught up with dissolves, voice-overs and gizmos. Just get the meaningful stuff out in front of those who would benefit from it.

BRING IN THE MARINES WHEN NECESSARY

There may be times when it makes sense to go outside and get third-party validation from a consultant or firm outside your organisation. This can be particularly effective if the issue you are tackling is profound enough to have a major effect on the performance of the site, either from a fiscal or technical standpoint. Politically sensitive issues may also call for this approach, particularly if your relationship with the decision makers involved is not well developed. There may also be times that the methodology called for is simply not in your arsenal.

For instance, I was once involved in a situation where two areas were fighting for the same limited real estate on the site. One side wanted to split the real estate in two, although the mental model of the customer would (I worried) see it as one. To make matters worse, they wanted to label the new separate areas with nomenclature that had everything to do with industry jargon and organisational charts, and nothing to do with customer expectations. And they wanted to do it right before the all-important Christmas shopping season!

Millions of dollars were at stake. I went outside and worked with a firm to develop a modified (and somewhat complicated) card-sorting and reverse card-sorting methodology to test both paradigms. In the end, the customer spoke, both sides accepted the result, and the site went on to have a record-breaking Christmas performance. It cost me a good portion of my research budget to do this, but the end result was worth it.

CULTIVATE EACH SILO INDIVIDUALLY

You will find that, in even the best organisations, people naturally identify with others in the same reporting chain or functional group. This can lead to wonderful cross-pollination, or to projects being tossed over the wall from one group to another with minimal interaction. Introducing the tenets of a sound user-centred methodology is going to be met with different reactions from different groups. As a usability person, your job is to develop a sound working relationship with each group, and to use your unique perspective to synchronise and harmonise their activities.

Sometimes the group can be tough to penetrate. In these cases, it may be prudent to seek out one member of the group who you feel may be the most open to trying out your ideas. Offer to do a project for them. In my case, an entrée into a relationship with the marketing group came from allying ourselves with the person responsible for outbound emails.

We tested some different approaches and the email guy was happy with the results. This gave us the ear of other members of the group, and the relationships built. Success also breeds success, so some well-placed tactical projects that you feel will be 'wins' can also get the positive buzz started. We leveraged a well-received checkout rewrite project to gain credibility with the IT group.

MAKE SURE YOU CAN DO IT WITH AVAILABLE RESOURCES

As a smart usability professional once so wisely said to me when I was contemplating a consulting job that was a total can of worms, 'Why associate yourself with something you know will fail?' Do not over-promise, do not oversell, and do not take on a project without confidence that you can see it through on budget, on time, and produce meaningful and credible results. If it fails, usability will get the blame. You can do without the 'agita'.

CULTIVATE VENDOR RELATIONSHIPS

This is another point to make: as a manager, you must cultivate and nurture relationships with vendors and consultants whose performance has a direct impact on your performance, and therefore on your comfortable retirement. In the past, these relationships have traditionally been adversarial: beat the vendor down in price. Let them know who's boss. In this day and age of supply chains and instantaneous data sharing, those businesses that forge solid and mutually beneficial vendor relationships, built on trust, will edge out the competition. Sometimes these consultants will be wellsprings of learning for you; other times, they can be your best job networks.

I've already described the relationship we had with our search vendor; another example for me was the relationship we developed with a well-respected Dallas usability lab. When we were building our own lab (and therefore reducing the business we'd be throwing this firm's way in the short term), the firm's president actually had his engineer come over and help us with our set-up. Why? Because he knew the importance of relationship building. He continues to be a friend and mentor to me, and Penney continues to have a productive relationship with him. So it paid off for both parties.

YOU WON'T HAVE ALL THE DATA YOU NEED. GET OVER IT.

Despite massive dollars being thrown at it and lots of vendors jockeying for market share, path analysis and this thing called 'clickstream' continue to be the Holy Grail. Nobody has a lock down handle on it, except maybe Amazon, and they're far from perfect.

As a usability practitioner, you'll be constantly challenged to provide the ROI. How did your efforts affect the business? Did you raise conversion? Did your putting that little 'view all' on the gallery pages work? Did your suggested name change from 'missy careerwear' (customer: blank stare) to 'office clothes' (customer: 'Oh, yeah') have an effect? Are you adding VALUE?

Answers to these are tough to come by, since any movement in the business is not the direct result of any single aspect of the site. It's a holistic, living mass of impressions, tools and opportunities. It might be your little improvement, or it might be a particularly effective email campaign or a particularly good performance day for the Internet 'backbone'. Customer service logs, emails and service reps can be a good source of data if you can't get anything directly from analytical tools.

There are any number of good articles by respected usability practitioners available on measuring the return on investment for usability. Some are a little far-fetched, but some may have value for you. Be sure you and your management champion (or boss) decide upon the appropriate ones for you.

In any case, use what you can and keep a good dose of scepticism around. Numbers can be made to say anything. This does not mean that you do not need goals and benchmarks to strive for; it merely means that you should utilise only those that you feel that you (and your boss) understand well and can trust.

LOVE YOUR JOB

Enthusiasm is infectious. People like to be around intelligent people with a real interest in what they do. Whether you came up through academia, technical writing, marketing, or wherever you sprang from, yours is a new and unique position with a singular opportunity to bring actual happiness to people. Really! Make the most of it, keep reading and learning, and socialise usability. Make it part of the culture within your organisation.

REFERENCES

Nielsen, J. (1994). *Guerrilla HCI: Using Discount Usability Engineering to Penetrate the Intimidation Barrier*. Retrieved from www.useit.com/papers/guerrilla_hci. html

Spool, J. (1999). *Why On-Site Searching Stinks*. Retrieved from www.uie.com/articles/search_stinks/

Spool, J. (2003). *The Quiet Death of the Major Re-Launch*. Retrieved from www.uie.com/articles/death_of_relaunch/

Schaeffer, E. (2004). *Institutionalization of Usability: A Step-By-Step Guide*. Boston: Addison–Wesley.

CHAPTER 4

Redesigning the United States Department of Health and Human Services Web Site

Mary Frances Theofanos and Conrad Mulligan

In the autumn of 2002, the United States Department of Health and Human Services unveiled to the public a new web portal. Designed by a multidisciplinary team of web developers and content experts from across the Department, the HHS portal design is based upon current research findings in the field of web site design, validated through an iterative series of usability tests (Theofanos, 2004). Overseen by a group of usability engineers from the National Cancer Institute's Communication Technologies Branch, the HHS portal represents 'best in class' design of Federal web portals.

Creating a single 'face' for the eleven operating divisions of HHS (among them such well-known organisations as the Centers for Disease Control and Prevention, the Food and Drug Administration, and the National Institutes of Health) was a complex task that required a formal and rigorous design process, content savvy, and political sensitivity. We present here the process used to redesign the hhs.gov portal, the trials and tribulations of the design team, and real-world 'lessons learned' that can be applied to any web site design or redesign activity.

THE PROCESS

Creating a wholly new, wholly user-centric 'face' for a Department of 65,000+ individuals and hundreds of independent organisations – all with their own content and web sites – was a daunting task, and one that required a comprehensive and formal project plan to ensure that the design was completed in the allotted six-month time frame. Utilising existing resources to the greatest extent possible allowed the portal design team to streamline the schedule and reduce project costs.

THE CONTENT

When designing a portal web site for an organisation with more than 100,000 web pages, it is useful to keep two things in mind: (1) You'll never find everything you are looking for; and (2) all content is not created equal. Lessons learned by the portal design team will illustrate the difficulties in identifying and obtaining appropriate content, and some effective workarounds that will get your design team thinking not in terms of organisation charts, but in more natural terms of content categories.

THE POLITICS

Turf wars, personality conflicts, and other 'political' issues pervade large, diverse organisations like HHS. Designing a web portal brings them all to the surface. From conflicts over how much 'screen real estate' should be allocated to each organisation to overcoming the fear of organisational identity loss, the portal design team confronted a host of sensitive issues.

While some issues could be addressed through usability testing and the application of user-centred design methods, others required the intervention of higher powers, and some of the most intractable issues refused to be solved.

Finally, this chapter will illustrate a host of design process dos and don'ts that can keep you on track and keep most of the project stakeholders happy at the same time.

WHY REDESIGN HHS.GOV?

Approximately 116 million adult citizens are online in the United States. Eighty per cent of all adult Internet users in the United States (approximately 93 million individuals) have searched for health and human services-related information online (Pew, 2003; Chen and Siu, 2001). The importance of the Department of Health and Human Services' information and the size of the Department's constituency mandate that its information be accurate, timely, easy to obtain and easy to understand.

The Department's first attempts at an Internet presence did not meet this mandate: a variety of forces resulted in web sites that consistently failed users in their information searches. Rectifying this situation to create a user-friendly (citizen-centric in government speak) Departmental web presence was a process initiated and guided by HHS Secretary Tommy Thompson and facilitated by

Executive Branch direction (the President's Management Agenda), federal legislation (the E-Government Act of 2002 and Section 508 of the Rehabilitation Act), and the inexorable shift from paper-based citizen–government interactions to the e-government model of electronic interactions.

E-government is defined as the use by the government of web-based Internet applications and other information technologies, combined with processes that implement these technologies, to the:

- enhance the access to and delivery of government information and services to the public, other agencies and other government entities; or to

- bring about improvements in government operations that may include effectiveness, efficiency, service quality or transformation.

At the most basic level, the reason behind the hhs.gov redesign was simple – the existing site failed users. These failures were recognised by the Department's Secretary, his staff, web site designers, usability experts and lay users. Although these opinions were not quantified until the start of the redesign process, they were strong and consistent enough to spur the redesign. The site's failure was mostly attributable to the decentralised nature of HHS, and web site policies and processes being weak and inconsistent.

THE DECENTRALISED NATURE OF HHS

Because the HHS was so decentralised, the information on HHS organisation web sites was often inconsistent, conflicting, duplicated or outdated. (Historically, line organisations have traditionally thought of themselves not as HHS organisations, but as independent organisations.)

By incorporating the redesign as part of his 'One HHS' Initiative, the Secretary aimed to reduce the complexity of HHS and create a sense of 'oneness' among HHS organisations. The One HHS Initiative was intended to ease user access to information from the Department's constituent parts (i.e. well known entities such as the Federal Drug Administration and the Centers for Disease Control and Prevention), by shifting how the public views their roles within the Department. The redesign of hhs.gov was a key component of remoulding both the internal and external views of HHS.

WEAK, INCONSISTENT POLICIES AND PROCESSES

Web site policies and processes were weak and inconsistent. Due to the decentralised nature of the Department, there was little or no high-level oversight of web site design practices or content policies at the line organisations (CDC, FDA, etc.). By taking a fresh look at the entire web site management process during the hhs.gov redesign, the Department aimed to establish uniform web site policies and processes that would more-tightly integrate in the public mind the relationships between HHS and its line organisations. The Department also hoped that this initiative would help establish a 'brand' for HHS.

The transformation of the HHS web site, as one component of the federal government's e-government revolution, is the focus of this chapter. Creating web sites that make it easier to find and understand information on federal government web sites is key to the successful transition to a 'citizen-centric' e-government.

The Administration's mantra of 'three clicks to service' (users should be able to find what they want in three clicks of a computer mouse), federal legislation regarding accessibility, and Executive Branch decisions regarding e-government often require federal web site owners to re-evaluate their designs and information hierarchies to integrate and simplify their operations. However, the legislation and Administration guidance merely prescribe the outcome; they do not present a roadmap to success. This chapter presents the experiences of those who were responsible for the reinvention of the HHS Internet presence to meet the demands and rigours of federal legislation, Executive Branch e-government moves, and most importantly the user. Our findings and lessons learned can serve as a road-map to the successful design or redesign of web sites.

WHO REDESIGNED HHS.GOV?

The hhs.gov site was not redesigned in a couple of weeks by a few people sequestered in darkened offices. It was redesigned by a large, multidisciplinary team of individuals drawn from across the Department.

The team was led by executive staff from the Office of the Secretary, who reported directly to (and were directly held accountable by) Secretary Thompson. The team also consisted of representatives from the Department's Operational Divisions – FDA, CDC, NIH, etc. (these are the content owner organisations within HHS), web site programmers and designers from the

Department and Operational Divisions, and a team of usability engineers from the Communication Technologies Branch of the National Cancer Institute (with whom the authors were affiliated).

This multidisciplinary team was tasked with designing a usable, citizen-centric electronic 'personality' for HHS. Our tasks were multiple:

- test the then-existing HHS home page to quantify its usability;

- transfer our usability engineers' years of experience to those who would be designing the HHS portal;

- oversee the design of the portal prototypes (to nip usability problems in the bud, if possible);

- test the usability of the prototypes; and ensure that the usability principles were applied to the design of the final HHS portal;

- oh, and make it attractive … function drove the process, but form was important, too.

WHAT WE ACCOMPLISHED

The redesign of the hhs.gov portal was a success. As Table 4.1 and the 'before-and-after' images indicate (see Figures 4.1 and 4.2), applying a rigorous, user-centred design process resulted in a more attractive, less cluttered and topic driven, user-centric portal. These attributes allowed usability test participants to more than double their overall success rate, and in some cases realise a tenfold improvement in their ability to find information.

DRIVERS FOR THE REDESIGN

The United States federal government is in the midst of an e-government revolution that represents a paradigm shift in the relationship between government and citizens. The range and scope of activities for which citizens use the Internet is astounding. Looking for health and medical information is among the most popular of these online activities. Eighty per cent of all adult Internet users in the United States (approximately 93 million individuals) have searched for health topics online, and a recent poll of cancer patients indicated that 71 per cent had searched the Internet for medical information to supplement that received from their doctors (Pew, 2003; Cooper and Victory, 2002; Chen and Siu, 2001).

Figure 4.1   Home page of hhs.gov before redesign

Figure 4.2   Home page of hhs.gov after redesign

Table 4.1   Success rates on usability test tasks, before and after site redesign

Usability Test Scenarios	Success Rates	
	Before	**After**
You want to find a nursing home for a relative.	38%	88%
You want to know what diabetes is and how you can prevent it.	73%	94%
You want to know what housing organisations are available to help assist the homeless in your area.	13%	94%
You want to know the Fiscal Year 2001 budget for HHS.	71%	94%
Your cousin is considering a career in medical research and asked you if HHS offers financial aid to undergraduate students.	8%	88%
Average success rate	**41%**	**92%**

Although citizen-driven, e-government is affected and shaped by government-wide legislation and regulation and organisation-specific policies and mandates. In this section we examine the impact of legislation, regulation, policies and mandates on the creation and use of federal e-health web sites and the lessons learned during the development of the federal government's premier e-health portal web site.

We begin by looking at the three elements of the mandate for e-government in the United States:

- the President's Management Agenda
- the E-Government Act of 2002
- Section 508 of the Rehabilitation Act.

THE PRESIDENT'S MANAGEMENT AGENDA AND E-GOVERNMENT

Facilitating a rapid transition to e-government is a national priority in the United States that enjoys the support of the President and Congress. The President's Management Agenda (PMA) contains five government-wide initiatives; of particular importance to the e-health enterprise is the Expanded Electronic Government Initiative (E-Government Initiative).

The President's vision for the Initiative emphasises that 'government needs to reform its operations – how it goes about its business and how it treats the people it serves'. (OMB 2002a: 4) The mandate is that electronic government becomes:

- citizen-centred, not bureaucracy-centred

- results-oriented

- market-based, actively promoting innovation.

The Initiative is designed to move the federal government to an era of e-government that accelerates and streamlines service to citizens, that improves significantly the government's quality of service to citizens, and that improves generally the government's effectiveness, efficiency and customer service.

The Initiative covers the range of activities necessary to complete the transition to e-government. It is concerned with Government-to-Citizen (G2C), Government-to-Business (G2B) and Government-to-Government (G2G) interactions, as well as the infrastructural and cultural modifications necessary to realise the potential of e-government. The federal government's e-strategy contains the vision and the action plan for the Initiative – it is at once a report card, a resource for those creating the transition to e-government and a road map for future activities.

THE E-GOVERNMENT ACT OF 2002

The PMA's E-Government Initiative is supported by the E-Government Act of 2002. This legislation is designed to 'assist in expanding the use of the Internet and computer resources in order to deliver Government services ... for a citizen-centred, results-oriented, and market-based Government' (Public Law 107–347, 44 U.S.C. Ch. 36). The legislation creates a systematic approach to managing technology in the federal government and promotes:

- use of the Internet and emerging technologies within and across government agencies to provide citizen-centric government information and services;

- access to high-quality government information and services across multiple channels.

Importantly for the E-Government and E-Health transitions, the E-Government Act advocates a more citizen-focused approach to current government-wide information technology policies and programmes.

SECTION 508 OF THE REHABILITATION ACT

In 1998, the United States Congress, recognising that technology can interfere with an individual's ability to obtain and use information quickly and easily, amended the Rehabilitation Act to require federal agencies to make their electronic and information technology accessible to people with disabilities.

Section 508 was enacted to eliminate barriers in information technology, to make new opportunities available to people with disabilities, and to encourage development of technologies that will help achieve these goals. The law applies to all federal agencies when they develop, procure, maintain or use electronic and information technology.

Under Section 508, agencies must give disabled employees and members of the public access to information that is comparable to the access available to others. Section 508 establishes standards of performance for federal web sites, particularly where the design or operation of software applications and operating systems, web-based intranet and Internet information and applications, and video or multimedia products are concerned.

HOW IT ALL AFFECTED THE G2C INITIATIVE

E-health, as one component of the federal government's G2C activities, is the focus of this chapter. The objective of federal G2C transition activities (and e-health activities) is to provide one-stop, online access to information and services to citizens such that they can quickly and easily find what they need, and can access information in minutes or seconds, instead of days or hours.

Creating web sites that make it easier to find and understand information is key to the successful transition to 'citizen-centric' e-government. The Administration's mantra of 'three clicks to service' – users should be able to find what they want (be it information about recreation, government benefits, health or agencies) in three clicks of a computer mouse – often requires federal web site owners to re-evaluate their designs and information hierarchies (Enterpulse, 2002).

SETTING THE STAGE: PRACTICAL CHALLENGES TO THE E-GOVERNMENT REGIME

The federal government has not in the past been known as very citizen-centric. American folklore is rife with stories of telephones ringing endlessly on government desks, of rude or unhelpful bureaucrats, and of seemingly endless hoops through which one must jump to obtain information. While some of this lack of citizen-centrism can be attributed to human resources issues, much of it is a function of the federal system itself. We look here in particular at three practical challenges to creating useful, usable e-government in the United States:

- the government's complicated physical organisation is mirrored in the Federal Web;

- the language of the bureaucracy makes comprehension difficult for citizens;

- Americans are a diverse citizenry with diverse needs.

GOVERNMENT'S PHYSICAL ORGANISATION MIRRORED IN THE FEDERAL WEB

Two hundred years of bureaucratic evolution have resulted in a vast federal government – fifteen major departments and hundreds of agencies, bureaux, institutes and other organisations, each with countless offices and branches, and within each a range of responsibilities and expertise. The ad hoc nature of bureaucratic evolution has resulted in overlapping briefs and activities within and between these major organisational structures – it is not unusual for several organisations to create, collect and disseminate information on a single topic, nor is it unusual for this compartmentalised information to conflict in some way (OMB, 2002a).

Unfortunately, the federal Internet presence ('federal web') has evolved to mirror the federal organisational structure, and first iterations of the federal web were confusing to citizens (Andersen, 2002). The first iteration was characterised by bottom-up development – web sites were largely created and maintained at the sub-departmental level, with little department-level oversight or direction.

This ad hoc, unstructured development process has resulted in a federal web that today contains an estimated 22,000 web sites with 35 million individual pages. The pervasive compartmentalisation of information on the federal web presents very serious information accessibility consequences, as it forces citizens to think not in terms of the information they want, but rather in terms of what organisations they think might hold that information.

THE LANGUAGE OF THE BUREAUCRACY

Bureaucracies create their own languages. While sentences composed largely of acronyms and abbreviations may enhance communication among insiders, such writing is not at all accessible to, or understandable by, the general citizenry. The need to make government documents more citizen-centric was addressed as early as the late 1970s, and the results of more than thirty years' work can be seen in today's much-easier-to-read government publications (Keane, 2002).

Federal web sites are particularly susceptible to the use of bureaucratese as web designers attempt to create dense, information-rich web sites and pages. In addition, many documents that were created for internal government audiences in pre-Internet times have been converted and posted to web sites, adding to the nomenclature problems of the federal web.

DIVERSE CITIZENRY

Americans differ widely in educational achievement: 16 per cent of Americans do not have a high school diploma or equivalent, while 27 per cent of Americans possess a Bachelor's degree or higher. The 1992 National Adult Literacy Survey indicates that 50 per cent of Americans read at an eighth-grade level or lower (U.S. Department of Education, National Center for Educational Statistics, 1992).

Americans do not necessarily speak English fluently: 18 per cent of Americans speak a language other than English when at home; 8 per cent of Americans speak English less than 'very well'.

Nearly one in five Americans over the age of five is classified as possessing a disability:

- 9.3 million Americans possess a sensory disability involving sight or hearing.

- 21.3 million Americans possess a condition that limits basic physical activities.

- 12.4 million Americans possess a physical, mental, or emotional condition that causes difficulty in learning, remembering, or concentrating (U.S. Census Bureau, 2000).

These statistics meant that we had to be very careful when talking about 'the user'. In reality, we couldn't really talk about a single user – we needed to recognise the spectrum of users.

THE REDESIGN PROCESS

As we have mentioned earlier, the redesign of the Health and Human Services web site was driven by four goals:

- Significantly improve the usability of hhs.gov, making it more citizen-centric.

- Create a visually appealing portal that is at once sufficiently governmental and approachable by a variety of users.

- Strengthen the 'branding' of the Department by reinforcing in the public mind the roles of the Department and its well-known line organisations such as FDA and CDC, among others.

- Meet the mandates of the 'One HHS' Initiative, the President's Management Agenda and Section 508 of the Rehabilitation Act.

The redesign process began from the premise that the then-current HHS home page was not meeting the needs of the average citizen. At the start of the redesign project, this was merely a considered opinion widely held by the Department's usability engineers, web site designers and staff from the Secretary's office.

To verify or challenge this opinion, we set about creating a design process that would (a) identify what features or design attributes of the then-current HHS home page were helping users and which were failing users, (b) establish through usability testing why these features or design attributes were failing users, and (c) address (a) and (b) in a new, usability-tested, user-centric design.

We chose this design approach for several reasons:

- First, the data collection activities allowed us to rapidly become familiar with the users and the users' terminology, to gain invaluable insights into what information the users were seeking, and to discover the types of problems that they encountered during their searching or browsing activities on the original HHS home page.

- Second, the iterative nature of the 'test and make changes' process allowed us to create a performance benchmark (or baseline) using the original HHS home page. This benchmark was then used to measure improvements in user performance when working with prototypes of the HHS portal.

- Finally, the iterative usability testing process allowed us to understand what features were useful to users, and what features were ignored, overlooked or improperly used.

DATA COLLECTION

Our rigorous design process demanded a detailed understanding of the failings of the original hhs.gov web site. To rapidly gain this understanding (we didn't have the luxury of time during the redesign process, so every step in the process was planned for maximum efficiency), we:

- Interviewed HHS and Operational Division executive and senior management, end-users, and other stakeholders to ascertain their opinions of, and experiences with, the original hhs.gov web site.

- Reviewed 246 email messages sent to the HHS webmaster and more than 16,000 email messages sent to the Office of the Secretary to identify typical user problems and concerns.

- Examined web server logs and more than 4,600 search engine log entries.

- Studied 292 responses to an on-line customer satisfaction survey.

- Evaluated 14 Cabinet-level home pages, Firstgov.gov, and Whitehouse.gov to ascertain user expectations.

These data collection and analysis activities provided invaluable insights into the users and their information needs, behaviours, terminologies and expectations:

- Interviews: The overwhelming majority of interviewees felt that the original HHS home page was not user friendly and that information was obscured and hidden by web site features and organisation.

- Server log analysis: The most-requested page on the old site was the HHS home page. The next most-requested page was the search page. This suggested to us that the navigational scheme on the HHS home page was failing many users. Users couldn't find the information they wanted on the home page, so they were resorting to the search page.

- Search log analysis: Almost 20 per cent of search queries were resubmissions of previously entered information or blank entries, indicating that users were having problems with both the search results returned by the web site and the search engine itself.

- Home page analysis: Current design trends have conditioned users to expect large numbers of links on the home page and to expect that those links will be visible (not hidden in a drop-down box, as they were on the HHS site).

Our initial data collection activities provided some insight into what web site features failed users, but we had no understanding of why particular features or design attributes failed users, the magnitude of the failings, or the interactions of the individual failure points. To gain this understanding, we conducted a usability test on the original hhs.gov home page, with the primary goal of establishing a performance baseline against which we could measure our progress during the redesign process.

THE BASELINE USABILITY TEST

The baseline usability test was conducted using 20 age- and ethnicity-diverse participants exhibiting a range of educational, socio-economic, professional and computer-experience backgrounds. Test participants included members of the general public, health professionals, Congressional staffers and rural health centre clients.

During the baseline test, each participant worked with us individually for one hour. During that time, the participants answered questions about what the site covered, its sponsorship, and intended audience; used the site to attempt up to 20 scenarios; and answered questions about their reactions to the site. The facilitator administered the scenarios in random order (that is, each participant completed the scenarios in a different order). Participants were instructed to complete the scenarios without searching, except during one scenario that specified the use of the Search function.

During the baseline test, we observed and recorded the following quantitative data:

- time to find the information (maximum allowed per scenario was 3 minutes);

- number of clicks;

- number of errors (defined as use of the back button or other change of pathway);

- success (completed the scenario).

Participants were instructed to complete the scenarios as quickly but as accurately as possible. Participants were not told to think out loud, although some did on their own. Our reason for not using 'think aloud' was to avoid any interference of thinking out loud with speed of finding the information.

Participant success rates in completing a selection of these scenarios are shown in Table 4.2. The scenarios in Table 4.2 are ones that were used in both the baseline and final testing.

We show these because we have direct comparisons on these scenarios. The average success rate for these scenarios (41 per cent) matches very closely the overall average for all 20 scenarios in the baseline test, which was 46 per cent.

The baseline usability test revealed some interesting insights about the web site, as discussed here and shown in Figure 4.3:

- Most participants were not successful in completing the scenarios.

Table 4.2   Success rates for five baseline test scenarios

Scenario	Success Rate
You want to find a nursing home for a relative.	38%
You want to know what diabetes is and how you can prevent it.	73%
You want to know what housing organizations are available to help assist the homeless in your area.	13%
You want to know the Fiscal Year 2001 budget for HHS.	71%
Your cousin is considering a career in medical research and asked you if HHS offers financial aid to undergraduate students.	8%

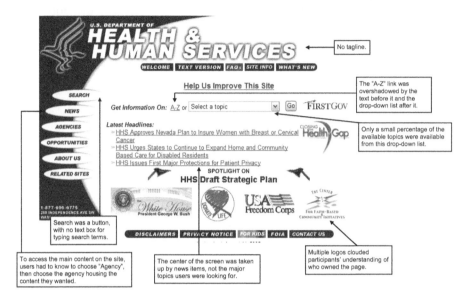

Figure 4.3   The original HSS home page, with problems and issues highlighted

- Participants tended to stay with a single information-finding approach. They did not use the multiple navigation features available on the site.

- Most participants were drawn to the 'Select a topic' drop-down box, even though it contained only a very small number of the many topics that HHS sites cover.

- Some participants thought the drop-down box was the place to type a search request.

- Only one user went to the 'A to Z' list. At the end of the session, we asked 11 people who had not used the 'A to Z' list if they had noticed it, and what they thought it was. Of those 11;

  – seven said they did not see it (four of them thought it was the same as the 'Select a topic' drop-down).

  – two said they saw it but it didn't register with them.

  – one thought everything was alphabetical (the drop-down was, so this person may really fit into the 'didn't see it, same as drop-down' group).

  – one thought it was the search box even though she did not actually type in it during the session.

- The logos at the bottom of the page clouded the participants' understanding of who sponsored/owned the home page. They thought the organisations displayed in the logos were sponsors.

- Participants felt that the home page was more 'health' oriented. They did not feel it had as much of a 'human services' orientation.

Our previous data analyses had indicated that nearly six out of every ten visitors to the HHS site could not find the information they were looking for. The confusion we witnessed during the baseline usability test was consistent with the previous analyses. We theorised that if we presented topic areas on the home page, users would get a better sense of the depth and breadth of HHS activities, and would thus be able to start immediately on a correct path to the information for which they were looking.

PROTOTYPING AND ITERATIVE TESTING

Our baseline usability test uncovered which features of the HHS home page were useful to users and which were failing them, and in so doing established that the existing site did not meet the needs of the user. Knowing how users wanted to find information was only half the battle, however. This is because a highly-usable information hierarchy and navigational structure is mostly useless if the topics contained within that hierarchy and structure don't 'resonate' with the user.

We continued by performing iterative usability and accessibility testing. We recruited 54 age- and ethnicity-diverse test participants for three tests. The participants represented a range of educational, socio-economic, professional, and computer-experience backgrounds. These participants worked through a set of scenarios similar in nature to those used during the baseline usability test (some of the baseline scenarios were carried over, and some new scenarios were created to test the emerging navigation scheme and categories, or 'channels').

Participants were asked to complete defined tasks in each of the scenarios, and to 'think out loud' during the testing. Participants were given the scenarios in random order. Each participant was accompanied in the testing facility by a trained facilitator who was responsible for leading the participant through the testing process.

During the test sessions, half of the participants were asked prior to working through the scenarios to describe the information they expected to find when clicking on a channel on the portal page. This exercise was conducted to evaluate how well the participants understood the channels, the 'resonance' of the channel titles, and the utility of placing a bulleted selection of content terms immediately below the channel titles. Then they were given the scenarios in random order and asked to use the 'think out loud' protocol during testing.

TUNING INFORMATION CHANNELS

Discovering as we did during the data analyses and baseline usability test that users prefer topic-based hierarchies to organisational-based hierarchies is no real revelation. Very large organisations such as HHS conduct such a breadth and depth of activities that even Departmental 'insiders' are often hard pressed to find information when it is 'stovepiped' (or kept in 'silos') according to organisational 'owner'.

However, reorganising a stovepiped organisation-based hierarchy into a topic-based hierarchy was not an insignificant task. No one before had attempted to organise HHS information topically rather than by organisation.

We faced two primary challenges in forcing this paradigm shift in how users view the Department's information (and, not insignificantly, how the Department views its own information):

- identifying what information to place on the portal's pages;

- determining the appropriate wording of these channels of information to be placed on the home page and the second level pages.

The first challenge was actually a two-part problem: The first part was identifying what categories (or 'channels') of information belonged high in the hierarchy. The second part was deciding what topics, pages or sites to place in those channels.

Because HHS is such a huge organisation, we often ran into problems with two or more groups 'owning' similar or identical information. Often, it made no sense to include both (or all) of the topics in the same bucket – the portal was supposed to reduce user confusion, not increase it by making them choose from one of two (or more) similar-sounding pages or sites.

The second challenge was especially delicate because no one ever had the temerity to lump together HHS information in the manner in which we were attempting, and consequently no one had any idea what to name the channels.

To create and name the channels, we conducted an informal card-sorting exercise. A team of more than a dozen health information experts – doctors, health policy professionals, and researchers, among other professions – created a vocabulary of commonly used terms by combining their expert knowledge of medical terminology with key terms extracted from the data collection and analysis efforts, keywords found on web sites across HHS and terms spoken by participants during usability tests of other HHS web sites.

The terms in this group were then placed on cards – one topic per index card – and sorted by the design team, resulting in groupings of like items.

These card-sorted channels were then populated with content terms gleaned during an intensive examination and 'mining' of myriad HHS web sites by the usability engineering team, other portal design team members and content experts from HHS Operational Divisions. These content experts were invaluable in creating and populating the channels as they possessed a detailed understanding of their own Operational Division's content – an understanding that we could not replicate given the tight timeframe of the HHS portal project.

TRYING OUT THE CHANNELS

Following the development of the channels and their content terms, a prototype of the HHS portal was created for use in a series of subsequent usability testing.

The first usability tests focused on ascertaining the performance of users when working with our channels. The channel titles were revised based on what we learned during the first usability test.

The second round of usability tests focused on the performance of users when working with the revised channels and their content terms. The results and feedback of this usability test were then used to further modify and improve the channels and content terms in preparation for the third usability test. Prototype pages incorporated few graphic treatments in order to minimise user distraction during testing.

As Figure 4.4 shows, the final portal design presents information and navigation topics in user-centric groupings, not in groupings driven by agency content owners.

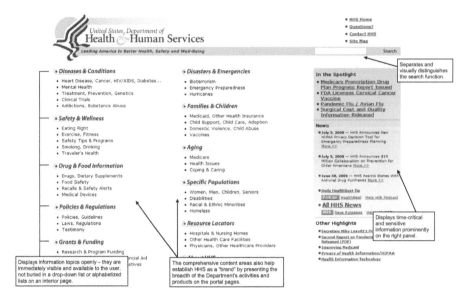

Figure 4.4   The redesigned HHS home page

These groupings do not force the user to work within an unfamiliar organisation-based information model. In addition, the portal:

- Displays information topics openly. The topics are immediately visible and available to the user, not buried in a drop-down list or in an alphabetised resource list as on the original HHS home page.

- Establishes HHS as a 'brand' by presenting the breadth of the Department's activities and products on the portal pages. Branding the site is accomplished by eliminating or reducing content owner-based stovepiping – in essence, Operational Division information is co-opted by HHS while maintaining the content's original ownership.

- Separates and visually distinguishes the search function.

- Displays time-critical and/or sensitive information prominently in the right panel.

- Removes confusing logos and other graphical elements to allow the user to focus on the topics and content.

VISUAL APPEAL AND BRANDING

Usability testing the HHS portal prototypes revealed significant performance gains compared to the original HHS home page. The new hierarchy made significant steps toward the branding of HHS and toward providing users with an understanding of the breadth and depth of HHS products and activities.

To build on this progress, we helped develop and test two separate treatments designed to enhance the visual appeal of the HHS portal. These treatments were designed to:

- communicate the timeliness, credibility, 'healthiness', and completeness of the HHS portal and its content;

- create a positive response to HHS among users;

- communicate to users the 'who, what, when, where, why and how' of HHS.

The treatments differed in the presentation of the HHS organisational logo. One treatment presented a colourful, flowing, stylised impression of the HHS shield, while the other presented a more-formal impression. Figure 4.5 shows the two logos.

The two treatments were presented to participants after they had completed the scenarios during the third usability test. Participants were shown both treatments and asked for their impressions. Nearly two-thirds of participants preferred the stylised organisational logo treatment that is found on the HHS portal today.

LESSONS LEARNED

The testing and redesign effort described above taught us these very important lessons:

- *Users come looking for topics.* However, the HHS home page did not present any links to topic areas – topics were hidden in the drop-down list and under the A to Z list.

Figure 4.5   Two visual treatments: informal (left) and formal (right)

- *Users can be confused by controls and icons.* Some participants thought the drop-down box was a search engine entry field. Only one participant figured out that the 'A–Z' icon would actually take her to a comprehensive listing of topics.

- *Nomenclature is king.* We witnessed radical improvement in user understanding of the information hierarchy when we used familiar terms and user-focused classification of terms.

- *Choices need to be clearly presented.* By not burying topics under an A–Z list and not obfuscating topical information behind an alphabet soup of agency and organisation acronyms and abbreviations, we realised significant improvements in user performance.

- *Imitation is the sincerest form of flattery.* The portal design team 'stole' some design ideas from other Federal portal-like sites, and we're not ashamed of it. The design ideas we stole allowed our site to mimic other Federal sites. This mimicry not only allows our site to meet users' expectations of a Federal site, it helps to reinforce positive user expectations. In sum, the new HHS portal 'looks' like what a user would expect a Federal web site portal to look like.

THE CONTENT

With a user-friendly, citizen-centric navigation scheme ready to go, the portal design team turned to identifying discrete content to link to from the portal pages. As designed, the HHS portal is only two layers deep: the top level domain and the tuned channel pages. Most links from the channel pages direct users to a line organisation (content owner) web site that is not within the hhs. gov domain.

Herein lies the challenge of content … HHS owns virtually no content. The folks that are researching cancer cures don't wear HHS badges. Nor do the folks that work to safeguard medicines or fight disease outbreaks. They wear badges from NCI or FDA or CDC. And the information that they generate is posted on NCI or FDA or CDC web sites, not on an HHS web site.

The Department of Health and Human Services is functionally an umbrella organisation. It represents its line organisations in the President's Cabinet, provides a funding avenue from Congress to its line organisations (like FDA, CDC, NIH and others), and addresses domestic and global health and human services policies for the nation in addition to accounting, legislative liaison etc.

However, most visitors to the HHS web site want to know about the activities of the line organisations, not find contact information for the Director of the Office of Competitive Sourcing.

The strength of the Department emanates from its Operational Divisions. Likewise, the strength of the hhs.gov portal is drawn from the strength of the Operational Divisions' web sites. However, because HHS doesn't 'own' or control these web sites, the portal design team faced a considerable challenge in identifying suitable web sites at the Operational Division level.

FINDING CONTENT

Finding content appropriate to link to, from the hhs.gov portal, was not quite a 'needle in a haystack' challenge … it was more of a 'needle amongst several hundred haystacks' challenge.

The Department of Health and Human Services is exceedingly complex – 300 separate programs, 65,000+ employees, and over eight million web pages. This complexity means that no single individual or group of individuals has a comprehensive understanding of what content can be found on the Department's web pages.

To overcome the challenge of complexity, the portal design team relied on distributing responsibility to its Operational Division representatives. These representatives were tasked with identifying suitable content that could be linked to, from the portal's tuned channels.

This arrangement provided several benefits: it allowed for rapid identification of suitable content by relying on individuals who were already familiar with the scope and content of their Operational Division web sites. When difficulties arose in identifying suitable content, these representatives knew who within their organisations to ask for help; this also helped to speed the content-identification process. This arrangement also allowed the Operational Divisions a great deal of control over what content of theirs would be linked to, from the portal; the importance of this is covered in more detail in 'The Politics' section below.

VETTING CONTENT

Finding content is only one part of the content challenge: vetting content is perhaps the more-difficult part. As Operational Division representatives gathered proposed content, the portal design team faced the daunting task of deciding what content would be linked to, from the portal pages, and what would not.

The vetting process can be a charged affair, especially when items from competing organisations are being considered for inclusion, and only one item will be chosen. To minimise the amount of upset caused by the vetting process, the design team focused their efforts on the quantifiable (ensuring equality of content) and leaving the qualitative decisions (suitability; political, cultural, moral sensitivities; picking one winner from a group of equals) to senior executive staff from the Secretary's office (see 'The Politics' section below).

Not all content is created equal. It was no great surprise that given the massive collection of web sites from which the portal design team could choose, web sites were selected that differed in quality, detail, scientific rigour and a host of other variables.

To ensure that all links from the portal pages represented the best information that HHS has to offer, potential web sites were evaluated by the entire design team to ensure that the language and detail was appropriate for the target audience (you don't link to information about clinical trials from a channel intended for children); that the sites were appropriately rigorous (in the case of channels tuned to researchers or doctors that require scientific rigour); and that the overall quality of the web sites was equivalent. Lack of consistency in overall quality – for example by presenting poorly-designed sites alongside well-designed sites – may cause the reader to question the accuracy of the information. This is unacceptable for a portal site dedicated to communicating health, medicine and human services information.

VERIFYING CONTENT

HHS content is constantly changing – new research discoveries, new studies, new policies and legislation, and emerging health concerns all conspire to keep HHS content in a state of flux. In addition, HHS Operational Divisions are constantly updating and changing the content on their web pages to keep abreast of these changes. This presents two primary content-related challenges: ensuring that web sites linked to, from the portal pages, present the most accurate, up-to-date information; and ensuring that the portal page does not become a graveyard of dead links as Operational Divisions create new content pages and move or remove old content pages.

The design of the HHS portal took six months. In that time, it was the responsibility of the Operational Division representatives individually, and the portal design team collectively, to continually verify the availability and currency of pages linked to, from the portal pages.

THE POLITICS

Politics – the inter-office kind, not the party political kind – was an ever-present spectre during the hhs.gov portal redesign process. Politics were sometimes overt – personality conflicts that threatened to slow the team's progress – but were more usually covert. Long-standing competition between Operational Divisions sometimes complicated the content selection process, for example.

Because politics are likely to complicate any governmental web site redesign process (or any redesign process that involves more than one individual, regardless of the content), we present here some of the challenges that politics presented, and some of our solutions.

ORGANISATIONAL EVOLUTION AND THE INERTIA OF BUREAUCRACY

The Department of Health and Human Services, which traces its bureaucratic evolution to 1789, comprises a dozen primary Operational Divisions and hundreds of sub-organisations. Many of the Operational Divisions are well known by the public – the Food and Drug Administration (FDA) and the Centers for Disease Control and Prevention (CDC), for example – yet most citizens are unaware that they are part of the Department. Similarly, many organisations within HHS operate largely autonomously with little oversight or management from the departmental level. Problems found at the federal level are found at the Departmental level – overlapping briefs; uncoordinated activities; duplicated expertise.

This organisational culture and the bureaucratic politics complicate the efficient and effective dissemination of health information. Because organisations within HHS tend to think of themselves as autonomous units, information has traditionally been compartmentalised within these units. This compartmentalisation has resulted in numerous challenges:

- duplication
- contradiction
- inter-organisational competition.

DUPLICATION

The nature of the modern health industry – research, clinical trials, longitudinal studies, patient and doctor education, and the regulatory and legal frameworks within which all of it takes place – naturally leads to compartmentalisation of information collection and dissemination, which in turn leads to duplication. The Department is rife with databases that contain similar or identical information targeted for different audiences. HHS web sites also contain examples of numerous iterations on a common theme – a single drug development may be documented on FDA, NIH, and NCI web sites, and while the information may be very similar or identical, each occurrence fulfils a particular need and perspective.

CONTRADICTION

Contradictory information can be found across the Department's thousands of web sites. These contradictions can be accidental (e.g., outdated information not being removed from web sites when updated information is made available) or a result of the nature of the medical industry (current studies may refute earlier studies; what's good for the goose may not necessarily be good for the gander). Accidental contradictions can be damaging to public trust; so, too, can purposeful contradictions if they are not properly contextualised or explained.

INTER-ORGANISATION COMPETITION

The compartmentalisation of the Department has created a zero-sum game – in an environment of steady or declining funding, compartmentalisation pits Operational Divisions against each other. These funding battles spill over into all other facets of bureaucratic life, resulting in unhealthy inter-organisational competition that must be overcome if information is to be provided to the public in an effective manner.

This competition extends to the Department as well – Operational Divisions can display a healthy suspicion of Department-led activities, fearing loss of control over their activities.

OVERCOMING INERTIA

The hhs.gov portal redesign team didn't have a whole lot of time to massage egos and find compromises – they had six months to radically reshape the public face of the Department. To ensure that they met their goal, the team quickly identified two key needs: obtaining executive-level support, and obtaining buy-in from the Operational Divisions. Without these two, the redesign process would have failed.

EXECUTIVE-LEVEL SUPPORT

A web site designer's best friend is an engaged executive-level champion – someone who recognises the importance of the web design or redesign process and who can 'make things happen'.

Executive-level champions should be seen by the entire organisation to be working through the design/usability team. The HHS portal design team was fortunate to have the executive-level imprimatur placed on them, and it proved essential to the success of the portal design process.

How and when the executive-level imprimatur is used is as important as the imprimatur itself. Learn from the little boy who cried wolf, and use your executive-level champion's power sparingly – executive-level champions should be a 'court of last resort' called upon to resolve only those issues that cannot be dealt with by the redesign team.

In the case of the hhs.gov redesign, executive-level champions were called upon to deliberate on issues of policy and content. Much of the work of Department researchers can be politically sensitive, depending upon whose political sensitivities must be considered. Thus, the design team turned to executive-level champions for the final word on what was politically acceptable for placement on the portal.

Similarly, the design team ran into 'screen real estate' concerns that it could not solve – in cases where limited screen space was available and multiple, equally-qualified links were in competition, the design team turned to the executive-level champion to decide what among equals would make its way on to the portal's pages.

By turning to an executive-level champion to make these decisions, the portal design team remained a neutral body that enjoyed positive, non-confrontational working relationships with Operational Divisions and others upon whom we relied.

OPERATIONAL DIVISION SUPPORT AND BUY-IN

The Operational Divisions possessed the power and influence to significantly hamper the redesign process. Recognising this, the portal design team worked diligently to obtain and keep the support and buy-in of the Operational Divisions.

Tightly integrating the Operational Divisions in the redesign process served to allay or reduce anxieties about loss of organisational identity, co-opting of information by the Department, and dilution of organisational identity. Getting Operational Division personnel involved in the redesign process and supporting the project was essential to success – without these individuals, it would have been impossible to identify suitable content or to design the concordance of terms upon which the natural navigation scheme rests.

SUMMARY OF OUTCOMES

The redesign of the hhs.gov web portal was undertaken to improve the ability of citizens to find and use information. The return on this investment is measured one citizen at a time – if the redesigned portal helps just one person find the information they need faster or more easily, then the redesign process has paid for itself.

Traditional return on investment calculations are a treacherous proposition for the HHS redesign project – HHS doesn't sell much (and sales certainly are not the primary driver of the web site), so the organisation cannot rely on 'sales' data to indicate the benefit/success of the redesign. On the cost side of the ledger, the complexity of the redesign process drew resources from across the Department and content owner organisations; this makes it very difficult to tabulate the actual labour cost associated with the redesign. Thus, HHS has no monetary 'benefit' data, nor any cost data, making a traditional cost-benefit analysis impossible.

To evaluate the 'return' on the redesign, HHS has used a variety of qualified and quantified performance metrics. Qualified information such as anecdotal evidence and informal feedback from internal and external users have been combined with quantified metrics such as site log queries to determine top pages hit, tracking of the use of the Search function, and usability test results to paint a picture of the 'return' to internal and external stakeholders. HHS continues to evaluate the web site design, and conducts web site usability tests when research findings of the public's interactions with the site indicate it is necessary.

ONE LAST LESSON

If there is one overarching lesson that the hhs.gov redesign team learnt, it is that 'data is king'. By gathering data on how users use the Department's web sites and scouring the body of research for data on how users use specific web site features, the team knew how to redesign the site for maximum efficiency.

By gathering data on the site's users, the team knew how to organise the site's content. Any by having this data readily accessible, the team could argue for good design in the face of politics- and preference-driven objections.

REFERENCES

Arthur Andersen LLP (2002). *A Usability Analysis of Selected Federal Government Web Sites*. Washington DC: Arthur Anderson LLP. (www.idt.unisg.ch/org/idt/ceegov.nsf/0/b99a279ceea247c5c1256c8a0054a387/$FILE/Usability.pdf)

Chen, X., and Siu, L.L. (2001). *Impact of the Media and the Internet on Oncology: Survey of Cancer Patients and Oncologists in Canada*. Journal of Clinical Oncology, 19, 4291–4297.

Cooper, K.B. and Victory, N.J. (2002). *A Nation Online: How Americans Are Expanding Their Use of the Internet*. Washington DC: National Telecommunications and Information Administration, U.S. Department of Commerce. (www.ntia.doc.gov/ntiahome/dn/)

E-Government Act of 2002, Public Law 107–347, 44 U.S.C. Ch. 36.

Enterpulse (2002). *The Internet Death Penalty: Most Web Visitors Never Return to Sites after a Bad Experience*. Retrieved from www.enterpulse.com/news/051502.html, December 2005.

Keane, K. (2002). Text of speech given by the Assistant Secretary for Public Affairs at the Interagency Forum on Plain Language, November 21, Washington DC. www.plainlanguage.gov/hotstuff/pl-forum-keane-speech.htm)

Office of Management and Budget, Executive Office of the President (2004).

Performance and Management Assessments, Budget of the United States Government, Fiscal Year 2004. Washington, DC: Office of Management and Budget. (www.whitehouse.gov/omb/budget/fy2004/pma.html)

Office of Management and Budget, Executive Office of the President. (2003). *Implementing the President's Management Agenda for E-Government: The 2003 E-Gov Strategy*. Washington, DC: Office of Management and Budget. (www.whitehouse.gov/omb/egov/2003egov_strat.pdf)

Office of Management and Budget, Executive Office of the President. (2002a). *E-Government Strategy: Simplified Delivery of Services to Citizens*. Washington, DC: Office of Management and Budget. (www.whitehouse.gov/omb/inforeg/egovstrategy.pdf)

Office of Management and Budget, Executive Office of the President. (2002b). *The President's Management Agenda, FY2002*. Washington, DC: Superintendent of Publications, S/N 041–001–00568–4. (www.whitehouse.gov/omb/budget/fy2002/mgmt.pdf)

Pew Internet & American Life Project. (2003). *Health searches and email have become more commonplace, but there is room for improvement in searches and overall Internet access*. Washington DC: Pew Internet & American Life Project. (www.pewtrusts.com/pdf/pew_internet_health_resources_0703.pdf)

Section 508 of the Rehabilitation Act of 1973, as amended 29 U.S.C. § 794 (d) (www.section508.gov/index.cfm?FuseAction=Content&ID=12)

Theofanos, M.F., Mulligan, C.P., and Redish, J.C. (2004). *Peak Performance: A New Approach to the Department of Health and Human Services Portal Gave More Power to the People*. User Experience 3, 4–7.

United States Census Bureau. (2000). *Census 2000*. Washington, DC: United States Census Bureau. (www.census.gov/main/www/cen2000.html)

U.S. Department of Education, National Center for Educational Statistics. (1992). *The 1992 National Adult Literacy Survey*. Washington, DC: U.S. Department of Education. (nces.ed.gov/naal/design/about92.asp)

CHAPTER 5

Creating Better Working Relationships in a User-Focused Organisation

Elizabeth Rosenzweig and Joel Ziff

We usability practitioners can be short-sighted: mistakenly assuming that everyone sees the world through our eyes. We know that when software, web sites and other high-tech products are designed in a vacuum, they often fail to meet users' needs and expectations. It's obvious to us that products fail if designers don't consider the perspectives, cognitive frameworks and culture of the intended users. We tacitly assume that everyone recognises the value of talking to users prior to designing the product, of testing prototype designs by having users interact with them so that we can learn from them before we commit time, energy, and resources to a final design.

All too frequently, it doesn't work this way in the real world. Though we practitioners know the value of our work, our colleagues don't always share our understanding and our commitment. They often conclude that our efforts to bring users into the design process are unnecessary, a waste of limited resources of time and money.

As we work to overcome this resistance, it is easy to mistakenly conclude that the problem can be solved by reason and logic. Our colleagues will accept our counsel if we can explain clearly what we are doing and why we are doing it; they will become allies if we can provide the objective data that show conclusively that a particular design is most effective. However, our colleagues are surprisingly not convinced by our research protocols or our objective results. The problem is not resolved by providing more data.

As usability professionals, we fall into a trap if we become narrow in our own vision and understanding. We will be frustrated and ineffective if we fail to appreciate the interpersonal dynamics at play in our own work environments, and how they affect the cooperative effort.

When we design and evaluate products we consider users' needs and motivations because that information helps us develop insight and design better solutions. We argue that usability practitioners can work more effectively with product management, marketing and engineering if we gain insight into our colleagues' experiences, perceptions, feelings and needs as well. We have found that usability professionals are vastly more effective if they seek answers to these types of questions:

- How do our colleagues perceive us?

- What are their beliefs about usability and user-centred design practitioners?

- What motivates them?

- What are their interpersonal strengths and difficulties?

- What is their experience of our work and us?

- Do they understand what we are doing?

- Do they think they already know how to design and resent our presence as designers?

- Do they feel threatened and intimidated?

- Is it hard for them to allow others to guide them?

- Do they feel a loss of control?

- Do they feel a need to impress their superiors so as to advance in their careers, or, in this era of uncertainty, to avoid losing their jobs?

- Are there pressures to shorten timetables or cut development costs?

When we understand our colleagues, we can use the knowledge to respond more effectively and efficiently to their concerns and issues.

In this chapter, we utilise a case study to explore some of the interpersonal issues that affect our capacity to be productive and effective in our work. We also identify some sources of resistance that usability professionals encounter, and offer a range of strategies for building a human–human interface by working collaboratively to find solutions that address these concerns. Although every encounter between professionals is different and requires a unique, creative response, we suggest a simple process as a framework for assessing the situation and creating effective strategies for overcoming problems (see Figure 5.1).

TAKE TIME OUT FOR REFLECTION

When we reach an impasse, we often need a time out, time to calm ourselves so that our thinking is not distorted by frustration, anxiety or hopelessness. How we do that is unique for each person, whether it be through diversion, physical activity, meditation, social support or other approaches to stress management. Most of the time, problems do not require immediate action. All of us have made the mistake of responding impulsively to an email or in a meeting, only later to wish that we could have expressed ourselves more thoughtfully and diplomatically.

When we feel ourselves at an impasse, it is helpful to take a breather, go for a walk, talk to a friend, play a game of basketball or do something that helps us to calm ourselves. After regaining our balance, we have an improved capacity to reflect and make sense of what has happened, to understand the challenges we face, and to develop creative strategies for overcoming those challenges.

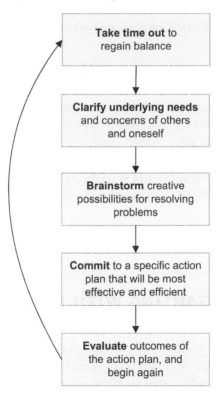

Figure 5.1   A framework for situation assessment and action planning

CLARIFY UNDERLYING NEEDS AND CONCERNS

We cannot develop effective strategies for overcoming problems unless we have a clear and accurate understanding of the underlying causes. Sometimes the reasons for resistance have been explicitly and directly communicated. Sometimes, personal, economic or technical issues are not expressed directly. Through reflection and/or discussion with others, we can gain understanding of these implicit concerns as a basis for devising effective strategies for addressing these issues.

BRAINSTORM CREATIVE STRATEGIES FOR RESPONDING TO UNDERLYING NEEDS AND CONCERNS

After assessing the underlying needs and concerns, we can brainstorm ways to address those issues creatively and effectively. Sometimes we can do that on our own. At other times, it is helpful to reach out to colleagues to help us in this process.

COMMIT

After clarifying an optimal strategy, it is important to commit to an action plan based on our assessment of which response may be most effective and efficient as a next step.

EVALUATE OUTCOMES AND BEGIN AGAIN

This process of reflection and redefinition continues. To the extent that our strategy has been effective, we confirm our hypotheses and build on that success. To the extent that our strategy is ineffective, we deepen our understanding of the underlying needs and how best to address them. Even if we learn that our assessment of the underlying needs is incorrect or that the strategy does not work, we have more information that allows us to do better the next time.

The dynamic nature of this process of ongoing self-reflection and learning is illustrated by the following case study.

AN EXAMPLE: STARTING WITH THE BEST OF INTENTIONS

A development group at a large corporation was given the task of designing a new home page for the company sales site. The company offered different versions of its product with different price points: a basic version at a lower price for the average consumer, and a higher-end version for business users.

The company decided to redesign its web site. After the budget was approved and the initial hurdles were overcome, the team was ready to begin the redesign process. The development team agreed to include a new recommendation engine on the web site.

Anita, an interaction designer, worked with Brian, a human factors engineer, to develop an initial strategy for implementing the recommendation engine. They undertook an ethnographic study as a basis for creating a low-fidelity prototype that could be tested with users prior to final design of the engine. This approach was an appropriate one, representing the most effective, cost-efficient way to create a design to best meet the needs of consumers.

However, their colleagues were not familiar with this approach. They encountered resistance when they presented their proposal to the team. Some of the team members dismissed the concept of an ethnographic study as a waste of time and effort, believing there were already enough data to know what to do.

Reluctantly, they agreed to allow the designers to go forward with their plan, waiting for the results of the ethnographic study prior to going forward with the final design. In retrospect, the designers erred by proceeding with the study, discounting the extent of their colleagues' concerns. They made the mistake of expecting their colleagues to be convinced by empirical research.

The ethnographic study revealed that many consumers were confused by the variety of products. Unsure of which product was most appropriate for their needs, they tended to delay making any purchase. Based on these results, Anita created an initial user interface design: a recommendation engine to help consumers determine which product to buy, based on responses to three simple questions. Although she wanted to test the design by sharing it with users and getting their feedback and reactions, she decided first to share the results with the team.

THE DESIGN PROCESS GOES AWRY

Anita called a meeting with Chris, the Project Manager; Debbie, the Marketing Manager; Ellen, the Web Developer; and Brian. Anita had a clear sense of her expectations: the meeting was to be a working session to review the results and the initial design. She neglected, however, to send out an agenda before the meeting, did not clearly articulate the goals and did not discuss her thoughts with anyone else.

Anita prepared a presentation. Although she had only six slides, she didn't get past the first one. Debbie interrupted Anita to question why they were doing so much work on this recommendation engine. Rather than using a recommendation engine to help customers decide which product was most appropriate for their needs, she wanted the web site to encourage consumers to buy the more-expensive products, thereby improving sales and profits.

Anita became frustrated and appealed to Chris to keep the meeting on track. Anita hoped that Chris would provide leadership to stay focused, reminding the team that the goal was to develop a design based on the results of the ethnographic study; however, he seemed reluctant to set limits with Debbie.

Anita did what she could to bring the focus back to the task of design, and was eventually able to finish her presentation. Anita then asked for feedback. Ellen raised concerns about implementation, leading to a lengthy discussion about technical issues. At the end of the meeting, Anita realised there had been no discussion of design issues. Frustrated but not wanting to appear negative and oppositional, she thanked everyone for coming.

LEARNING FROM WHAT HAPPENED: A SECOND ATTEMPT TO CONVINCE THE TEAM

After the meeting, Anita and Brian shared their frustration with one another. Brian complimented Anita on the way she maintained a professional and positive presence throughout the meeting despite the poor responses. Assessing the underlying issues, they concluded that the team meeting was problematic; creating a tone of negativity that was not constructive, not allowing time for one-to-one dialogue or for team members to understand the proposal and its rationale.

They developed a new action plan. They would obtain more consumer data, as originally planned, testing the recommendation engine using low-fidelity prototypes and prepare a report to be sent to team members, soliciting feedback via email rather than in a meeting. In this way, team members could have an opportunity to understand the concept and rationale more fully and to share their reactions individually. Anita and Brian could then follow up with individual team members as needed.

Anita made some low-fidelity prototypes based on the design criteria created as a result of the ethnographic study. Anita and Brian showed the low-fidelity prototypes to customers and asked for feedback. The reactions were varied, but most people were satisfied, even happy, with the notion of a recommendation engine. It appeared that this approach enabled customers to feel more trust in buying products on the web site. Anita and Brian summarised their findings in a final report that they sent to the team distribution list. They received no comments, and concluded that everyone was satisfied with the results, or, at least, had no serious objections. They believed they had succeeded in overcoming the resistance by changing the framework for communication: avoiding the unproductive forum of a meeting and utilising one-to-one communication via email. In retrospect, they would discover that they had made another mistake. They began to work on the final design based on their research.

Anita was happy with the final design and enthusiastic about the effectiveness of the process she had used, creating a design that integrated the feedback from customers. She felt confident that the rest of her team would also be impressed. She hoped that the positive outcome would not only affect the quality of this particular product, but would also establish her credibility and make it easier to get support in the future for incorporating usability research into the development process.

Chris scheduled a meeting to discuss the final design. Anita looked forward to the meeting, confident that it would provide an opportunity to validate her work. Later on, she would discover that her enthusiasm had blinded her, causing her to interpret the lack of response as acceptance of the proposed design.

However, Anita was not completely oblivious. Recalling how Chris had failed to take leadership in the previous meeting, Anita realised that she could not count on Chris to provide needed support in the forthcoming meeting. Chris had the responsibility for leading the meetings, was generally supportive of her work and had the capacity to focus; however, he had recently seemed distracted and overloaded. She decided to overcome this problem by talking with him prior to the meeting. She realised that he would not be open to criticism and might only become defensive or even hostile, but she decided to ask him for help. Chris was very busy and only able to schedule a brief phone meeting. Anita summarised what she had done, working to build support by sending out the report to team members and expressed confidence that there was more support for the new design.

Chris replied that he had not had a chance to review her report but was glad that there had been support from others. In response to her request for help keeping the meeting focused on the topic, Chris assured Anita that he would make sure that she had the opportunity to present her ideas.

ANOTHER IMPASSE: PRELUDE TO UNDERSTANDING THE UNDERLYING ISSUES

Chris opened the meeting by asking Anita to present her design, asking others to hold back comments until she was finished, after which there would be time for feedback. Anita was pleased that Chris had taken a stronger role as leader. She presented her design without interruptions. Anita was glad she had asked Chris to help the group stay focused. Everything seemed to be progressing according to her plan.

However, after she finished, Chris shared his reactions to the design. Chris did not like the new design. He believed that the current design was simple and worked well. He did not believe that the change was significant; moreover, he thought it was too risky to make a dramatic change from the current design.

What Chris did not say was that he wanted to create a high-quality product but was impatient. Chris also did not say that he had limited experience with, and did not understand the value of, usability research. Even more significantly, Chris did not speak explicitly about his personal situation: Chris had recently received a negative performance appraisal. He had been specifically criticised for bad judgement in some of his decisions. He knew the company was considering lay-offs, and he did not want to lose his job. He was reluctant to make a radical change: if it was not successful, it would provide further evidence of his bad judegment.

Ellen expressed concern about the schedule. As the developer, she had to do the programming to make it all work. She already felt overloaded and unable to meet her timeline. She did not want to add more work to her already heavy load. Ellen's concerns were not hidden: she had been clear and open expressing her needs.

Debbie attacked the design, focusing her comments on the first screen. She discussed, in great detail, every mistake and flaw in the design. What she did not say is that she continued to feel the same concern that she had previously raised. She did not see a need for the recommendation engine. She believed that it would undermine sales by guiding consumers away from the higher-priced product and saw no reason to spend money to reduce income. However, since she had previously raised this issue, she was reluctant to do so again.

Anita was surprised and frustrated at the negative reactions to her design. She did not understand why no one had responded to her when she had sent the design to everyone for review. She began to defend herself, reviewing her research findings, explaining why the design was correct.

Chris stopped her. He needed to end the meeting on time. He tried to address some of the issues by defining some action items to be completed prior to the next meeting in two days. He asked Anita and Ellen to meet and discuss the impact of adding the design to the current development schedule. He also asked Brian and Debbie to meet with him to discuss the issue of the recommendation engine and the impact upon sales.

Anita was very nervous about the meeting that Chris, Brian and Debbie had scheduled. Anita wanted to be there even though Brian could represent her interests at the meeting. She tried to talk to Chris after the meeting was over, but he was impatient with her because he was late for another meeting. Anita asked Chris if he would meet with her later that day. He was booked, but agreed to try to make room in his schedule to talk with her the next day.

LEARNING FROM WHAT HAPPENED: GETTING BACK ON TRACK

After leaving the meeting, Anita felt upset, realising that she had made a mistake when she believed that her contribution would be respected and supported. She was frustrated that she was not going to be able to move forward quickly to the next stage of implementing the design. She calmed herself by taking a long walk around her favourite lake. After she calmed herself down, she realised that she had allowed her own enthusiasm to colour her judgement and conclude that others would be equally positive about the design.

She resolved not to continue making the same mistake. She decided to meet with a colleague (who was also a friend) from another group to strategise how to proceed. After spending some time talking about her frustration and impatience with the level of resistance, her friend, who also knew Chris, helped her understand some of the underlying needs and concerns that were driving Chris, especially the effects of his negative appraisal.

Her friend also suggested that the action steps Chris had taken could provide a constructive forum for responding individually to address concerns of specific people. The meeting with Ellen could allow Anita to work to resolve her issues. The meeting with Chris, Brian and Debbie could be a useful forum if Anita could also participate. Anita arranged to meet Ellen later that day, and got Chris to agree to include her in the meeting with Debbie and Brian.

ADDRESSING ELLEN'S CONCERNS

Anita and Ellen met to review the design. Anita started by encouraging Ellen to talk about her concerns. In doing so, Anita demonstrated that she had learned from her previous mistake. Rather than trying to 'sell' to Ellen, Anita encouraged Ellen to speak about her concerns. Ellen expressed concerns about the time required for programming the recommendation engine. She did not want to make extensive changes to the design, but instead wanted to add a button for the recommendation engine and let the user have an option to use it. Also, Ellen explained that it was not technically possible to implement Anita's suggestion.

As a result of listening more fully to Ellen, Anita was now able to respond more effectively to Ellen's concerns and create a foundation for gaining her support. Anita reassured Ellen that she recognised the difficulty of making changes that required substantial time spent in programming and affirmed that a solution was required that was practical to implement. Anita also responded to Ellen's suggestion, explaining that the solution of providing a button to access the recommendation engine did not accomplish the goal of guiding the consumer more effectively since many users would bypass the button.

However, she also acknowledged the technical and practical concerns that Ellen had raised. Anita offered to explore some ways to address both these concerns and asked Ellen to give her some time to discover other solutions. Ellen was relieved to have Anita's help and glad to be able to work on other tasks in the interim. Although the issues had not been resolved, Anita felt confident that she had established a better working relationship with Ellen. She appreciated Ellen's concerns and also felt that Ellen understood her goals. Anita was now empowered to work towards finding a solution that would address Ellen's concerns while also accomplishing Anita's goals.

MARKETING MEETING WITH CHRIS, BRIAN AND DEBBIE

Anita felt a high level of distress prior to the marketing meeting with Chris, Brian and Debbie. Chris acceded to Anita's request to attend the meeting, but only with the agreement that Anita refrain from engaging in active conflict and allow Brian to respond to issues raised by Debbie. Chris did not directly explain his reasoning, but Anita knew that Debbie controlled the funding for the project and that Chris was afraid that Anita would be too aggressive with Debbie.

Although Anita knew that it was important for her to respect Chris's request, she realised that it would not be easy to keep quiet. Anita had strong feelings about her design. She wanted her design to be accepted. She believed that the design would help consumers make educated decisions. It felt like a violation of her personal integrity to manipulate or mislead people and encourage them to spend more money buying a high-end product that they do not actually need. Anita was frustrated and angry that others, especially Debbie, did not share her values. She wished she did not have to expend so much energy convincing others to consider ideas that Anita believed were not only self-evident and the right thing to do, but also ideas that, in the long term, made good business sense by establishing the consumer's trust in the company. She wished she could just work on design issues and not have to spend so much effort convincing others to accept her ideas. In recognising her own needs and concerns, Anita understood the challenge she faced in maintaining a low profile. With this awareness, she was more able to control herself at the meeting.

At the beginning of the meeting, Chris asked Brian to explain the results of his study to Debbie. Brian explained that his work was not a marketing study, but rather an ethnographic study. Through interviews with consumers, he focused on qualitative rather than quantitative data that provided insights into users' unmet needs. Although the conclusions were not based on large numbers or on statistical data, they were nonetheless significant based on industry guidelines that validated this type of research. In-depth interviews with a small number of consumers provide a depth of understanding of qualitative issues that are not always evident in statistical and quantitative analysis. Many of the consumers interviewed expressed a need for help figuring out which product was appropriate for their needs. Many of them were so confused by the choices that they went to the web sites of competitors whose products were more clearly described and differentiated.

Debbie responded by reiterating her concerns regarding the marketing issues and profit margins. Based on her analysis, she believed that it was more cost-effective to focus on selling the higher-end product: even if some customers were lost due to frustration with the web site, it would be offset by the higher profits generated by the more-expensive product.

Anita, with difficulty, kept her promise to listen and not respond while Debbie shared her concerns. Chris summarised the issues and ended the meeting without any resolution but assured Debbie that he would continue discussions with Anita and Brian to clarify how to address her concerns.

STRATEGISING TOGETHER: TURNING CONFLICT TO COOPERATION

Anita realised that she could not implement her design without agreement from Debbie. However, Debbie was under pressure to maximise short-term profits: she had no incentive to achieve long-term, less-tangible goals such as building consumer trust and brand loyalty. Although Anita did not know how to solve the problem, she did now have a better sense of Debbie's concerns and recognised that regardless of the results of her studies, Debbie had no incentive to buy in to Anita's proposal. She did not know how to implement the solution, but she did know what had to be done to gain Debbie's support.

Anita decided to meet privately with Chris to explore possible solutions to this problem. Anita hoped that they could find a way to change the metrics that were used for calculating the marketing managers' pay. Instead of basing their pay solely on sales, Anita proposed adding another metric based on customer satisfaction. Chris liked the idea but was pessimistic about the practicality of implementing this kind of change. However, he suggested that Anita prepare a short paper documenting how attention to usability and customer satisfaction might affect short-term buying decisions as well as long-term customer loyalty. Anita agreed to this plan and sent the proposal to Chris the following day.

Convinced by Anita's summary of the issues, Chris decided to take the proposal to the company Leadership Team. Chris reviewed the proposal with Debbie who was excited by the idea. The conflict between Debbie and Anita had been defused. If this proposal was accepted, Anita's efforts to improve usability would have the potential to increase Debbie's income rather than reduce it. Anita, Brian and Debbie worked together to prepare a revised pay system that included a customer satisfaction metric.

The Leadership Team, who had previously established customer loyalty as a company goal, accepted the proposal as consistent with their mission. The remuneration package for marketing was revised to include a customer satisfaction metric. Moreover, in making this proposal, Chris, with Anita's help, had gained personally as well, establishing his leadership with his peers and superiors.

On a parallel track, Anita worked with Ellen to resolve some of the technical issues regarding programming. Anita researched the issue of including an intelligent engine in the web site and found a paper from MIT outlining the steps needed to implement this feature. Based on this information, Ellen agreed, in principle, to the concept but was still concerned that the programming of the feature would add four weeks to her schedule. Anita suggested that they take this issue to Chris for a final decision. Chris wanted the new feature to be included and asked Anita and Ellen to find a way to make it possible within the deadline.

THE NEXT GROUP MEETING: RESOLUTION OF ISSUES

At the next team meeting, Chris asked each of the team members to update the team regarding the status of the web site redesign. Ellen reported that she had resolved the technical issues and would be able to implement the design but that it would still require additional time to complete.

Debbie reported that she now supported the concept of the recommendation engine because it would increase customer satisfaction. She wanted the design to be implemented in time for an upcoming trade show. Chris complimented Anita on working with the team to overcome the hurdles. He established a committee to focus on the timeline and resources needed to complete the redesign in time for the trade show.

ANALYSIS OF THE CASE STUDY

Anita initially made some serious mistakes. She was blinded by her own professional perspective, believing that colleagues would share her views about the process of design as a scientific endeavour in which data from customers would guide decision making. She also failed to take into account the unspoken but important concerns of her colleagues. Although potentially jeopardising her effectiveness, these misjudgements instead provided Anita with important information that allowed her to understand these unspoken concerns and to address those concerns so as to overcome resistance to her ideas.

Mistakes are inevitable as we respond to complex and changing dynamics, often accompanied by pressures of limited time and energy. However, if we learn from our failures, we will not continue to make the same mistakes and will often be able to find constructive solutions to impasses that seem initially to be impossible to overcome.

WHAT WE CAN DO: RESOLVING INTERPERSONAL IMPASSES

There are a variety of approaches that can be used to overcome the interpersonal challenges that occur in work relationships. These are pictured in Figure 5.2 and described below.

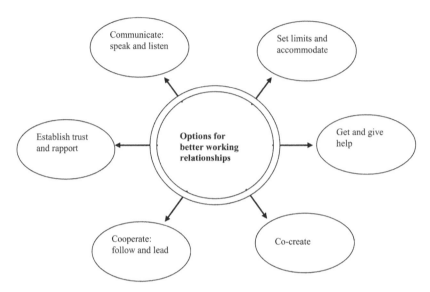

Figure 5.2   Techniques for creating better working relationships

ESTABLISH RAPPORT AND TRUST

Resolution of impasses requires a foundation of rapport, trust and sense of shared mission so that everyone involved is willing to communicate their thoughts and feelings, to understand one another's concerns, and to work together to overcome differences. Anita discovered a breakdown when she encountered hostility and negativity in her initial meeting with the team. She attempted to remedy the problem by switching to one-to-one individual communication via email.

Although her assessment was correct, the strategy did not work because team members disengaged and failed to respond. Recognising this problem, she shifted to direct face-to-face conversation with her peers. This approach worked for her. In some situations, there is a deeper personal disconnection, requiring that we build a better base of connectedness.

In some situations, our means of communication is problematic when we use email or other indirect communication, instead of a more-direct method. In other situations, there is a systemic breakdown in which trust and sense of shared mission is missing. It is not easy to change these situations. But we have a greater chance of overcoming the problem if we recognise that it exists, and at least know what we need to change.

COMMUNICATE

Impasses in the design phase often result from miscommunication, failure to express ourselves clearly or misperceptions of others' perspectives. By focusing on listening and speaking more effectively, we may discover that the differences are not as significant as we imagined.

LISTEN

Prior to making efforts to have colleagues understand our perspectives, it is important to take the time to listen, to understand colleagues' perspectives. Listening not only requires that we give the other person time to speak, but involves actively encouraging them and helping them to clarify what they think and feel.

We also have to pay attention to non-verbal communication and information received indirectly through other people. This approach not only helps us address their concerns but also builds trust and rapport. Anita and Brian made this mistake repeatedly when they attempted to explain their approach to other team members while ignoring cues that indicated resistance to their proposal. When Anita spent time listening, she understood more completely the concerns of other team members.

SPEAK THE LANGUAGE OF YOUR COLLEAGUES

When we do begin to communicate our perspectives, it is important to do so using language that makes sense to the other person. When we use technical language that is understandable only to us, our colleagues will, at best, be confused, and, at worst, withdraw or become hostile.

For example, although the concept of an ethnographic study made sense to Anita and Brian, other team members were not necessarily familiar with this type of study, and did not automatically accept it as a valid and constructive approach. We also need to verify that others understand our message and have not misinterpreted on the basis of their perspectives.

SET LIMITS

When we clearly know we are right, our willingness to take a stand can be very constructive. Even if we do not have all the authority, it may be that the strength of our integrity and the underlying correctness of our position enable us to persevere and succeed.

For example, Anita held her ground with regard to the best approach to design. She believed strongly in the value of basing design on studies of customers. She persisted in her efforts despite adversity and difficulty. Without that strength of will, she would have not ultimately have succeeded in her efforts.

ACCOMMODATE

There are times when we may be right but are powerless to get others to consider our proposals due to economic or personal reasons. When we face these realities, we recognise the need to stop fighting a battle than cannot be won. Accommodating graciously helps us retain goodwill and trust so that we can take the initiative at another time when we have more ability to have our ideas considered by others.

Anita faced this reality when she recognised that the first meeting had got out of hand. Rather than futilely attempting to get others to consider her ideas, she adjourned the meeting in a positive fashion rather than continuing to fuel the frustration and anger.

Similarly, when Chris gave Anita permission to attend the meeting with Brian and Debbie only if Anita agreed not to speak or become argumentative, Anita accepted his limit rather than challenge him. Interestingly, Anita, in doing so, gained from taking a less-active role, understanding Debbie's concerns more fully because Anita listened rather than argued.

GET AND GIVE HELP

Get help

We do not always have sufficient understanding or skills to solve all problems. Recognising when we need others, need their wisdom, guidance or encouragement, allows us to solve problems that would otherwise be overwhelming or result in our making serious mistakes. Anita recognised, in several instances, that she needed help. She sought the counsel and support of a colleague after she became frustrated and lost hope after her initial meetings.

Give help

In some situations, our colleagues are resistant because they need help. Perhaps they are overloaded and stressed, or perhaps they lack technical skills and are reluctant to admit that they are unable to do their jobs.

Anita achieved better cooperation from her colleagues when she responded to their personal and technical concerns, helping Chris to focus, helping Ellen to implement the new design, and helping Debbie to be more successful. Helping others is often a very important approach to overcoming resistance.

COOPERATE

Follow

There are times when we do not have the formal and/or informal authority to take initiative to resolve problems. Chris, for example, had the formal authority and responsibility for running meetings. If Anita had attempted to run the meeting and maintain the focus, she would have failed because she did not have the formal or informal authority to get others to comply. She needed to enlist Chris, as team leader, to accomplish that task.

Similarly, the decision to change the metrics for evaluating Debbie's job required advocacy by Chris to achieve that goal. She could provide him with the information he needed, but Chris had the authority and knowledge to define the process and strategy.

Lead

At other times, we do have the formal and/or informal authority to take the initiative to integrate different concerns and needs so as to resolve problems. Anita effectively took the lead in advocating that the design process be centred on the customer's experience. She gradually gained understanding of colleague's concerns and became more effective in creating a plan that addressed everyone's agendas.

Co-create

In well-functioning teams, each person works collaboratively with the other, respecting one another, working to understand different perspectives, and searching together for solutions that incorporate everyone's needs. In Anita's team, despite some initial problems, the underlying dynamic was a positive one in which people did work together.

As Anita helped to bridge some of the differences, the team was able to work together more constructively, with each person contributing unique expertise to help resolve problems. The result was heartening. The new design, created through collaborative effort, was much easier to use.

Users reported that despite some initial apprehension, they felt that the recommendation engine ultimately was helpful. One user commented that she was usually distrustful of computer-generated suggestions, suspicious of attempts to make her buy something she doesn't really need. Despite that scepticism, on this web site she experienced the process as honest and constructive, and thanked the designers for their integrity.

In this case example, we have described the dynamic, iterative process of ongoing dialogue, reflection and assessment that enables us to develop constructive and effective responses to human problems that impede the design process. As we take time to reflect upon a situation, we are able to identify ways in which we have responded rigidly and ineffectively.

With that understanding, we can clarify new approaches and strategies. Learning from our mistakes, we gradually become more effective in our interpersonal communication, enabling us to identify problems and resolve them more efficiently and effectively.

CHAPTER 6

Using Innovation to Promote a User-Centred Design Process While Addressing Practical Constraints

Leslie G. Tudor and Julie Radford-Davenport

What happens when two newly hired usability engineers are asked to provide usability support to a project whose domain is completely new to them, in a company whose culture and process is unfamiliar, for a first-release application with prospective users who are not easy to come by? These were just some of the challenges the authors faced when they began working on the Information Map Studio (IMS) project at SAS Institute.

Both of us had arrived at SAS Institute after spending the bulk of our professional lives working at Bell Labs and AT&T, respectively, where our concentration had been devoted to the usability of telecommunications and human resources software, as well as telecommunications hardware devices. After ten years of working exclusively in telecommunications, the field of business intelligence was one that we both found intriguing, but of which we had virtually no practical knowledge. (Business intelligence is a general term that refers to the process of leveraging all of the information at one's disposal to make better business decisions.)

The fact that our collective experience in the BI domain was lacking was made uncomfortably clear when we found ourselves assigned to a project that focused on the needs of business intelligence users, in a division where business intelligence applications were aggressively developed. Quickly getting up to speed was critical to the success of our contribution.

WHAT IS INFORMATION MAP STUDIO (IMS)?

IMS is an application that enables a fairly technical user to create a business view of physical data (that is, an 'information map') that is relevant to the analytical needs of business users who use reporting tools. The information map contains the basic data items in which business users are interested, along with filters that allow them to home in on the details. After importing the information map into their reporting-tool applications, business users can combine and re-combine data items, with or without filters, to answer new and evolving questions. Best of all, this can be accomplished without a middleman to translate the business needs into an appropriate database query.

Even a relatively simple information map can answer a variety of questions. For instance, an information map containing only seven data items (Store ID, Region, Product Line, Date, Order Number, Sales Amount and Loss Amount) and four filters (Store ID, Region, Product Line and Date) can answer all of the following sample business questions:

- What is the total sales amount for video games (the newest product line) this year?

- Which stores in the south-eastern region have the greatest total loss amounts?

- Does the total sales amount exceed the total loss amount for store 42?

- Which product lines are the most profitable?

- Which product lines are being sold in the south-eastern region?

- Which stores are in the south-eastern region?

- How do sales of the most profitable product lines compare across regions?

The key advantages of IMS for business users are that it is flexible in terms of the number of questions it can answer and timely in that users can immediately run queries specific to their business needs on demand. IMS also reduces the overall workload on information technology (IT) organisations that support these business users: rather than repetitively generating new reports that look at the same data from a slightly different angle, the IT organisation can focus on creating and maintaining information-rich maps that help business users answer their own questions.

THE CHALLENGES

We quickly ascertained that we faced these formidable challenges:

1.   There were no established customers or user contacts from whom we could readily recruit participants.

2.   The time available for meeting with users, conducting user needs analysis and gathering baseline assessments was limited.

3.   There was no prescribed process for communicating our findings to the development teams.

4.   We had limited subject matter expertise, complicated by a need to coordinate design efforts during the parallel development of first-release products.

5.   There was no explicit window of time in the software development life cycle reserved strictly for design activities.

How we responded to these challenges is the focus of our chapter.

OVERCOMING THE CHALLENGES: SOLUTIONS WITHIN CONSTRAINTS

NO ESTABLISHED CUSTOMER BASE OR USER CONTACTS

Almost immediately, we experienced the challenge of working on a first-release application developed for a sophisticated set of highly technical users with a unique skill set. This meant that prospective users were rather difficult to locate and recruit for usability-related activities.

In addition, several prospective customers identified by the sales and marketing groups were purchase-decision-makers and so not necessarily appropriate candidates for design work and usability testing. Finally, travel was limited due to various project-related constraints. As a result, we concentrated on locating local business intelligence experts who approximated the knowledge and skill set of our targeted end-user.

COMMUNICATING WITH CURRENT AND FORMER COLLEAGUES

We began identifying appropriate end-users by first approaching current and former colleagues who had ties to the community of users we were seeking to recruit. Our colleagues identified several internal contacts whose previous jobs had required them to both create and maintain business metadata. As internal co-located SAS employees, these contacts were able to devote a significant amount of their work time to sharing their knowledge and providing us with feedback.

These colleagues became invaluable in helping us understand the 'big picture', as well as the nuances of some of the more-complicated business intelligence issues. By querying former colleagues who had experience in data warehousing and reporting activities, we located two individuals who, throughout the design cycle, evaluated initial designs and provided us with user needs analysis data.

UTILISING OTHER BUSINESS CONTACTS AND THE INTERNET

Ultimately, all of the individuals we selected were obtained through contact with current or former colleagues. However, we also contacted instructors of business intelligence metadata courses and referenced online question and answer forums to identify potential users. After reading a number of postings, we found that there was a core set of active forum participants. We also discovered that these different methods often identified the same individuals.

In one case, a current SAS colleague identified a former colleague as a prospective user who also happened to be one of the most active participants on the online forums. Later, a local BI course instructor identified a former colleague as an excellent candidate for usability testing. As a result of this overlap, we felt fairly confident that we were able to generate a group of highly experienced and knowledgeable contacts out of this pool of potential 'informants'.

It is worth noting that almost all of these contacts were enthusiastic about participating in evaluation activities and interested in learning more about the application. Many also desired to maintain contact with us. Our 'home-grown' circle of contacts has been so useful, we're almost glad we didn't have a pre-established user group!

MINIMAL TIME FOR USER NEEDS ANALYSIS OR BASELINE ASSESSMENTS

A basic user interface framework for IMS had been implemented prior to our assignment to the project; however, very little background information about how the design was derived was made available to us. In addition, the development cycle was moving forward and our window of opportunity was rapidly narrowing. The pressure to immediately begin tackling major interface design and redesign efforts was growing but we knew that first acquiring a more-intimate knowledge of user needs was essential to the success of those efforts.

EXPLORATORY USABILITY TESTING

If we had had enough time and resources, we would have chosen to perform a task analysis, a technique used to understand the users' tasks and the aspects of their environment that promote or undermine the effective completion of those tasks. Instead we opted for conducting highly interactive and fairly lengthy usability testing sessions with a group of expert users. We asked participants to commit to a minimum three-hour session so that we would have ample time for discussion; however, most sessions ran an hour or two longer than scheduled.

The test sessions were conducted in the most convenient location for our participants: their homes, offices and, in one case, a hotel suite. Conducting the test sessions outside a formal lab reduced the overall level of experimental control during the test sessions; however, the more-informal environment proved to be especially conducive to fostering a relaxed, collaborative experience that could comfortably run significantly beyond the three-hour minimum commitment we requested.

At this point we were looking for information, not trying to confirm or validate a design. The scenarios that we asked users to complete were therefore very broad, general tasks. In fact, we only delved into details when the discussion naturally led us there or when the task was inherently complex. The tasks included adding/removing tables or cubes in a map, organising and renaming the contents of the map; creating a variety of filters, modifying relationships between tables and running test queries.

We instructed participants to use the 'thinking aloud' method (Nielsen, 1993), in which they voiced both positive and negative thoughts while working through each task. We also asked our participants to rate how easy (or difficult) it was to complete each task, and how confident they were that the task was completed correctly. Participants were asked to base their survey ratings on their actual experiences during task completion and not on their expectations of how easy or difficult it would be to complete the task again in the future.

The test sessions generated a wealth of information. Our initial summary was as follows:

- The original design had significant usability problems. We found several issues that stemmed from design decisions made shortly after the IMS project was conceived. Our development team recognised these as such, but changes had not yet been implemented due to resource constraints and the complexity of the changes that were required. This usability test helped to clarify these deficiencies.

- Our early-stage design decisions also posed challenges to users. As expected, the usability test also highlighted issues with our own early design work. Even our combined experience as usability engineers, comprising more than 25 years, was not enough to offset the lack of contact with representative users. The opportunity to conduct task analysis/field observations, and usability testing with low-fidelity prototypes prior to design would have provided us with a richer set of data from which we could have designed.

- Some users had difficulty learning and using certain less-familiar user interface controls.[1] Some of the functionality within IMS is designed and maintained by a specialised components team. These components are designed to meet similar needs for specific pieces of functionality across multiple applications. Some of the usability issues that surfaced during our test session had to do with the task flow integration of these objects into the IMS application.

- Participants wanted additional functionality. Because our participants were all business intelligence experts, they periodically expected to find and use functionality that had not yet been included in the application. A few of these issues were significant in terms of the resources required for implementation and in terms of the ultimate success of the product.

This exploratory approach to usability testing allowed us to gather a great deal of information quickly. Not only did we walk away with a laundry list of usability issues to address, but we also we had a much richer understanding of the business intelligence domain and our users' needs, including some possible new requirements.

FOLLOW-UP USABILITY TESTING

After most issues were fixed, we conducted a second round of usability testing. The goal of this testing was to assess the effect of these changes and to establish a usability benchmark so that we could set a reference point against which future performance would be measured. We were interested in learning whether our user interface changes would improve participants' task performance, so we decided to re-use some of the task scenarios from the first test.[2] Likewise, we

---

1   SAS has a strong emphasis on component re-use and projects are encouraged to use component objects when appropriate.
2   We did not re-test aspects of the user interface that had not changed significantly since the first test.

also returned to our original participant pool. We were able to re-test with four of the nine original participants.[3]

Radford-Davenport had previously conducted remote usability testing in her work at AT&T and found it to be an effective, low-cost means of gathering user data. Since we had already established professional relationships with our participants, we did not feel that it was necessary to meet in person with each participant a second time.

We conducted the usability test sessions remotely via Placeware Web Conferencing. This approach allowed the participants and the facilitator to interact with the application through a shared virtual desktop from the comfort of our own homes and offices. Unlike the previous lengthy test sessions, these sessions lasted only about an hour. As in the first usability test, participants were asked to indicate how easy each task was, and how confident they were that they succeeded at the task.

The results of the tests revealed that IMS had made usability gains on virtually every aspect of the user interface for which documented issues were addressed (see Table 6.1). The only exception to this occurred when the implementation of new requirements made the functionality much more complex. This information is, however, being fed into the next round of design efforts.

Participants also encountered some areas of the user interface that had been troublesome during the first round of testing, but had not yet been significantly improved. As expected, our participants again had trouble in these areas, confirming that the designs were inadequate and modifications were necessary. This confirmation of our original findings helped to expedite the recommended changes to the user interface.

NO ESTABLISHED PROCESS FOR COMMUNICATING WITH THE DEVELOPMENT TEAM

After completing the first usability testing effort, we looked forward to communicating our findings to the product management and development teams. However, our design and analyses were not part of the formal project

---

3   Several of the original participants were SAS employees who had been experimenting with IMS for use within their groups. We dropped those participants from the second round of usability testing to minimise the chance that any performance improvements would be due to experience with the product. Scheduling difficulties prevented us from utilising all of the remaining participants from the first usability test.

Table 6.1   Usability improvements for selected IMS tasks

Tasks	Usability Test 1	Usability Test 2
Renaming data items.	Participants expected a 'Rename' option in the context menu.	Participants easily found and utilised the new 'Rename' option on the data item context menu.
Setting data item properties.	Participants had difficulty understanding the significance of the Data Item ID field and how this field related to the Data Item Name.	No participant mentioned the Data Item ID field, which had been moved to a less-prominent position.
	Participants also did not understand the concept of having a single data item act as both a category and a measure.	No participant mentioned the classification of a data item (*either* category *or* measure now) as a point of confusion.
	Participants were confused by grouping box labels that contained options for allowing and restricting options.	No participant mentioned the new grouping box labels as a point of confusion.
	Participants objected to the default option of dynamically generating a list of data item values.	No participant objected to the new default option 'Allow user to enter value'.
	Participants could not always predict the purpose of the tabs that comprised the Data Item Properties dialogue based solely on the names of the tabs.	Participants could predict the purpose of the tabs based solely on the new names of the tabs.
Running a test query.	Participants had difficulty figuring out how to test their map once it was created.	All of the participants were able to easily locate the facility for testing their map.
Renaming a table.	Participants confused the functionality for renaming a table with the functionality for creating an alias of a table.	All of the participants were able to easily rename a table. No participant confused the goal of renaming with the menu option to 'Insert Alias'.

tracking system, so those teams had only vague expectations regarding the method and timing of our presentation.

In one sense, this was an advantage. It afforded us a great deal of flexibility. However, it did force us to think hard about the best vehicle for communicating our results. The various parties were interested in the specific parts of our findings that were relevant to their respective work agendas. For example, the developers needed to know specifically what changes should be made to better support existing functionality, while the marketing representative was more interested in learning about the requests for new functionality.

A single presentation in which all stakeholders were present would have been efficient for us, but not terribly practical for attendees. The developers, marketing representatives and user interface analysts would require a detailed level of analysis that allowed them to apply those data to their own requirement lists and design decisions. In contrast, upper management would desire a high-level readout.

In particular, the success of our presentation to development was crucial: the development team lead was compiling a list of 'most annoying IMS issues' from internal users as we were compiling the usability testing results. A compelling presentation would help to ensure that results based on feedback from representative users were weighted appropriately against other known issues. In order to help development attack these issues according to their impact on usability, a presentation that focused on an objective analysis of the data was required.

Customising the information to best meet the needs of the different groups that comprised our total audience was key. Therefore, we decided on a multi-faceted approach to communication and presentation, tailored to the needs of each stakeholder group. They are listed below.

EMAIL SUMMARY

The week after the conclusion of our last usability session, we sent an email to the IMS development team providing a high-level overview of the positive and negative aspects of our findings, as well as task-related user comments. The primary goal of this communication was to quickly deliver a digestible amount of input to the extended team. The email contained a brief hit-list of high-priority issues, cushioned by the many positive findings. This vehicle for communication enabled us to deliver a summary of results that was informative, interesting and concise.

MEETING WITH MARKETING AND COMPONENTS REPRESENTATIVES

Shortly after the last usability test was conducted, we met with our marketing representative to discuss findings that had an impact on current and future requirements. For issues pertaining to components, we met with the usability analyst of the components team. These individual meetings let us take specific issues directly to those individuals who could best address them.

USE OF EXISTING COMMUNICATIONS SYSTEMS

After generating plausible solutions to the problematic elements of the interface, we created associated defects, using a 'defects' application that allowed development to track internal bugs. The defect text that we entered included a detailed description of the problem, a criticality rating based on its overall severity, and suggested solutions. By working within the established mode of communicating software problems, we were confident that each of these defects would be resolved in some fashion.

USABILITY TEAM READOUT

IMS is but one application in a suite of BI tools, all benefiting from usability support staff efforts. Collectively, these usability analysts are responsible for designing the user interface for the entire suite of BI products. Therefore, we expected that a verbal presentation of our findings to this group would generate many questions, as well as a great deal of discussion.

Additionally, it would give the analysts an opportunity to jointly discuss the ramifications of these findings for their respective products. Indeed, this information formed part of the basis on which their future design decisions would be made.

USABILITY TEST REPORT

A few weeks after the last test session, we distributed a detailed usability test report to the entire extended team. This report summarised the qualifications of our participants, described the test procedure in detail, outlined the individual tasks, provided the qualitative and quantitative results and listed the associated criticality rating, defect number and status of all identified issues.

In addition, each of the usability issues found in the test session was described at length, often broken down into the steps that comprised a task, and specific recommendations were provided. Red text was used to highlight issues with high criticality ratings that had been deferred. To facilitate our readers' ability to scan the report for findings, we also captured screen images throughout IMS and annotated them with brief textual descriptions. These illustrations were indispensable to the readability of the report: readers could literally acquire an overview of the findings by simply reviewing these pictorial slides. Figure 6.1 provides an example of these images.

This multi-faceted approach has helped to assure that most of the issues we discovered during the initial usability test were addressed in some capacity.

Slide 18: Relationship Tab (continued)

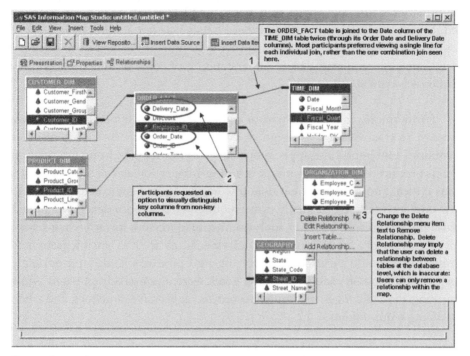

Figure 6.1   Sample slide used in the usability test report

Subsequent to delivery of the usability test report, the development team asked us to prioritise the deferred usability defects so that they could develop a long-term plan of attack.

For issues involving components, the usability analyst of the component team conducted a subsequent usability test to clarify the issues, address more-complex scenarios, and evaluate the functionality in a variety of product contexts. To date, the vast majority of the issues identified in the original usability testing have been addressed.

LIMITED DOMAIN KNOWLEDGE AND PARALLEL DEVELOPMENT OF FIRST-RELEASE PRODUCTS

The usability testing sessions and ongoing communications with the participants provided us with an abundance of data with respect to user needs and domain knowledge. We were also reading voraciously in an attempt to master topic-relevant information. However, even though our knowledge of the domain was rapidly evolving, it was still quite limited. We struggled with complex topics like OLAP/cube data manipulation and the consequences of creating a map with multiple inter-related tables. Though we did have several information-gathering phone calls with our BI contacts, relying on them to educate us about the intricacies of these issues was not an option, as most of our contacts were quite busy. Yet, in order to design for the next set of business requirements, acquiring a basic understanding of some of the more-complex issues was critical.

Furthermore, as IMS was part of a suite of business intelligence tools, we needed to ensure that the design of IMS would support the needs of users working with reporting applications to generate reports from information maps produced by IMS. Creating a seamless integration across these products was critical and added a great deal of complexity and coordination effort to the implementation of virtually every requirement, for both development and usability. As a result, usability analysts attempted to work towards a consistent prioritisation of complementary requirements, as well as an integration of design that would ensure that reporting tool products could appropriately expose information map data. These goals were aggressively pursued while meeting the challenges of limited resources, aggressive timelines and often evolving requirements.

As a first step to designing for new functionality, low-fidelity paper prototypes were created. In order to successfully evolve preliminary designs, feedback from all the major stakeholders was desired: developers, marketing representatives, usability analysts and representative users. Obtaining feedback from the usability analysts that supported other SAS BI suite products was particularly important since, like IMS, many were also first-release products.

Tudor had previously conducted domestic and international participatory design sessions using both the PICTIVE (Muller, Hallewell Haslwanter and Dayton, 1997; Muller, Tudor, Wildman, White, Root, Dayton, Carr, Diekmann and Dykstra-Erickson, 1995) and CARD (Tudor, 1995; Tudor, Muller, Dayton and Root, 1993) approaches for a variety of applications. These approaches consisted of involving users in early design work of desktop and auditory applications. In the PICTIVE approach, actual users generated low-fidelity designs using a combination of sticky notes, markers and transparency paper.

During CARD sessions, task flows were presented by laying out minimised versions of screen shots which allowed users to perceive the overall gestalt of one or more sets of flows. Tudor had found that the design ideas generated from these sessions were pivotal in evolving existing designs and providing direction for new designs.

We initially thought about holding such a participatory design session, using our paper prototypes as a point of reference for session design work. However, because of scheduling conflicts, it was quite difficult to organise a series of these sessions.

We also considered conducting usability test sessions with these paper prototypes. We have each done extensive one-on-one testing using low-fidelity prototypes in the past and found this to be an extremely efficient way of getting user input at the early stages of the design process (Snyder, 2003). However, in this case, a more participatory, group-based effort was desired, since key participants had their own unique domain knowledge that could be shared with others in the context of a design session. It was the sharing of this knowledge that we thought might affect the design in ways that one-on-one testing could not.

In her work at Bell Labs, Tudor conducted low-fidelity testing using a whiteboard upon which was affixed a series of prototyped screen shots representing specific user scenarios for a telecommunications application. This approach was a variation on the CARD methodology that Tudor discovered (1995) in which playing cards, each containing a card-sized screen shot, are displayed on a flat surface, allowing users to see the gestalt of an entire task flow.

As with the CARD methodology, displaying eight-inch by eleven-inch screen shots on a whiteboard allowed participants to get a sense of the full task flow in a way that could not easily be replicated by interacting with a live application, and also allowed users to interact with the display by affixing sticky notes directly to the screen shots. Based on Tudor's experience with this method, we expected that this approach would be beneficial for IMS as well. We ultimately opted to use a variation of this approach to gather input from the diverse and busy members of our mostly co-located team.

ASYNCHRONOUS COLLABORATIVE DESIGN

Rather than scheduling a standard participatory design session, we invited the development team, the usability analyst community, marketing and management to provide input via an asynchronous collaborative design process. We were fortunate in that some of these participants' former responsibilities were consistent with those of our target users. Using large whiteboards that were mounted near our respective offices, we posted paper prototypes, along

Figure 6.2   Asynchronous collaborative design hallway display method

with step-by-step scenarios describing how each new piece of functionality would be utilised (see Figure 6.2).

The boards were hung in relatively quiet side-hallways to afford the participants some 'thinking space'. Instructions were emailed to participants, who were asked to review the prototypes at a time most convenient to them. Participants utilised the sticky notes, different coloured pens, and scrap paper to post comments and alternative design ideas. These comments, suggestions and alternative design sketches then became part of the foundation from which each subsequent participant viewed the prototypes.

To help foster an interactive experience, participants were also encouraged to respond to other postings. The result was a dynamic and evolving conversation about the design possibilities. Table 6.2 lists some advantages of the asynchronous collaborative design method.

Most participants spent approximately 30 minutes completing this task; however, a number of participants were observed for an hour or longer reviewing the prototypes and providing feedback. These users reported that they enjoyed the process so much that they simply were not aware of the time spent critiquing, reading other people's responses and responding.

Because participants were not required to schedule a time for task participation, several participants arrived at the whiteboard while other

Table 6.2   Advantages of the asynchronous collaborative design method

Advantage	Elaboration
Diversity of input.	Feedback was gathered from a variety of people with different roles and domain expertise (including developers, marketing representatives, managers, testers, documentation specialists, user interface analysts) from within and across product teams.
Improved buy-in.	The asynchronous collaborative design method improved buy-in for the entire IMS usability effort. Because multiple prototypes were often included for the same slice of functionality, participants became aware of the design trade-offs as a by-product of contributing to this process.
Reinforced teamwork.	Participants from development, marketing and management thanked us for involving them in this process. One manager thanked us for the great 'team-building' effort, expressed that she had never been asked to contribute to a design before and indicated that she was delighted to have the opportunity to do that. A few developers told us that they were shocked that we were asking them to provide input to the design, and thanked us.
Increased awareness of usability.	Because the sessions took place in a public space, surrounded by offices that were occupied by employees representing various disciplines, and who supported a variety of projects, we received many inquiries about the task. Comments such as, 'I didn't realise that this was the type of stuff you guys did' and 'This is great! Can I participate too?' made us realize that this was not only an excellent way to collect user feedback, but also an effective way to campaign for usability.
Showcased our work.	As a beneficial by-product of this exercise, our personal design work received a great deal of exposure. A wide spectrum of co-workers, including management, developed a new (or renewed) appreciation for the complexity of the design task, as well as the collaborative approach we were promoting.
Served as a valuable communication tool.	In many instances, the designs conveyed information to participants about issues that we did not even know existed. For instance, usability analysts and managers from related products noticed and were able to communicate inconsistencies in the ways that the same slice of functionality was being presented across products.

participants were completing the task. In many cases, participants discussed the pros and cons of various design alternatives with each other and had insights that they might not have had otherwise.

NO EXPLICIT DESIGN TIME IN THE DEVELOPMENT LIFECYCLE

Once the second wave of marketing requirements was received, the development team immediately began evaluating the technical effort required to implement the new functionality. Likewise, we began to scope the anticipated design effort for each of the new requirements and fed that information to the development team for use in prioritising new work.

Due to the deadlines we were working against, unless design efforts commenced immediately we risked losing the one opportunity that would allow us to get ahead of the curve: once the cross-product priorities were established, all of our design efforts would occur in tandem with development. An accepted risk of this approach was that we would invariably begin designing functionality that would ultimately not be prioritised for the next major release. Given the amount of ground we had to cover, it was critical that we iterate quickly.

By this time, we had a greater mastery of the BI domain, but still required input from a variety of sources in order to evolve the designs rapidly. We considered emailing a PowerPoint slide packet of the designs to participants, or posting the designs on the SAS intranet. Although, logistically, each of these approaches would have been easy for us to implement, we were concerned that our designs might languish unopened in participants' in-boxes or that participants would not feel compelled to visit an intranet site where our designs were posted. Most importantly, the collaborative flavour of the task would be lost.

While considering the best method for gathering additional input, we also noted that the prior utilisation of the asynchronous collaborative design method had not been without its drawbacks. One of the few disappointing events during the initial trial was that several management-level employees were not able to participate, due to time constraints. Additionally, we recognised that the prior round of testing did not allow us to interact with the users as they performed the task. For the future, we desired a more personal interaction with the participants as they reviewed the prototypes, so that we could engage them in discussion, ask clarifying questions, and, in general, get as much information from our participants as possible. We settled on two compromise approaches that, individually, addressed both of these concerns.

MORE ASYNCHRONOUS COLLABORATIVE DESIGN: THE 'ROLLING WHITEBOARD' APPROACH

In an effort to make management participation more convenient, we settled on the notion of a 'whiteboard on wheels' that could be rolled into management offices (see Figure 6.3). A three-foot by five-foot long board was procured and proved to be ideal – due to its relatively small size it was easy to transport and participants did not object to its presence. The fact that the board was two-

Figure 6.3   Asynchronous collaborative design rolling whiteboard display method

sided was also advantageous as it allowed us to post prototypes on both sides of the board, one scenario per side.

After working with a scenario posted on one side of the board, the board could be turned to work with the remaining scenario. After each participant completed the entire task, the designer retrieved the board and transported it to the office of the next participant. Each participant had the benefit of reviewing the sticky notes of those who participated before them. In all other respects, the task was not much different from having participants come to the static whiteboard, other than making it extremely convenient (possibly even unavoidable) for them to complete the task and eliminating the likelihood that more than one participant would show up at the same time.

In contrast to the static whiteboard approach, this approach required the physical effort of transporting the whiteboard to and from various management offices. However, this small drawback hardly nullified the advantage that this method afforded. By bringing the whiteboard to the users, we were able to overcome time constraints that would have otherwise prevented management from participating.

Furthermore, the rolling whiteboard was ultimately used in ways that were initially unanticipated. In one case, after participating in the task, a participant recommended that we both replace and enhance a dialogue box with a specific component. Further discussion about this issue resulted in a brainstorming session with the components team usability analyst, as well as a subsequent meeting with the entire components team, in which the mounted designs and the sticky notes they contained were used as a point of reference.

EVEN MORE ASYNCHRONOUS COLLABORATIVE DESIGN: DESIGN BY APPOINTMENT

To increase the amount of interaction between the participants and designers, we used yet another asynchronous collaborative method to gather feedback for additional slices of functionality. Again, as in the first round of asynchronous collaborative design testing, some of our participants' former responsibilities were consistent with those of our target users.

For this approach, designs were posted on multiple pages of an easel pad and on a large whiteboard that were located in one of the two authors' offices (see Figure 6.4). The large whiteboard was ideal for displaying designs that represented more-ambitious functionality requirements, while the easel provided an appropriate surface for less-complex designs. Unlike our original sessions with the publicly displayed board, participants were scheduled to begin the task at specific times.

We found that during these one-on-one sessions, most participants were eager to engage the designer in discussions about various aspects of the design, functionality and design alternatives. In fact, these conversations often yielded significantly more qualitative data than the sticky notes. It appeared that participants preferred verbal communication and so were less inclined to record their comments.

As a result, recorded comments did not always contain the full spectrum of information communicated to the designer during the session. To ensure that the goals of an evolving collaboration amongst participants were achieved, the designer recorded verbal feedback on additional notes that she then placed alongside those generated by the participant and affixed to the prototypes. In this way, each succeeding participant could benefit from the many ideas voiced or written by those who came before them. It's important to note that,

Figure 6.4   Design by appointment display method

even though there were many positive aspects associated with this method, the need to record user comments in this way made this a more labour-intensive procedure for the designer.

Another time-intensive aspect of this procedure was that these were 60- to 90-minute sessions that required the presence and often the participation of the designer. The designer's scheduling constraints and these somewhat lengthy, individualised sessions resulted in a smaller number of participants than did our original process.

Ultimately, the development team provided many valuable insights into how the design could be improved. The participants reviewed design prototypes for six discrete yet highly interrelated aspects of the application, recording their comments on sticky notes and annotating the designs with these. This feedback helped to evolve the designs in a matter of days when otherwise it might have taken weeks to achieve the same level of input and integration.

Unlike a design readout, which typically results in only minor tweaks to an otherwise-finished design, this process truly capitalised on the unique knowledge of each person on the team to rapidly iterate to a sophisticated set of designs. The collective impact of this feedback cannot be overestimated: in many ways capturing this input early helped to ensure that the designer did not spend a lot of time and energy pursuing a design path that would ultimately not be feasible or that would need some degree of redesign before the next release.

NEXT STEPS: ELECTRONIC ASYNCHRONOUS COLLABORATIVE DESIGN SESSIONS WITH CUSTOMERS

Having both recently acquired additional responsibilities, the time we can devote to the IMS product is even more constrained than before. Yet we do not want to finalise our designs for new functionality without input from representative users. Our respective time constraints, coupled with our strong user-centred design philosophy, have motivated us to create methods for gathering user input efficiently, without abandoning the collaborative approaches that have worked so well for us.

Table 6.3   Advantages and disadvantages of different asynchronous collaborative design techniques.

Prototypes posted...	Advantages	Disadvantages
1. ... in a hallway.	- high exposure - good PR opportunity, showcases UCD - participants enjoyed the activity - facilitated discussion between participants.	- management is less likely to participate - less opportunity for clarifying communication with participants .
2. ... on a rolling whiteboard that was moved from office to office.	- target participants, particularly management, are more likely to participate than in #1 - participants enjoyed the activity - participants appreciated the convenience of participating in the comfort and privacy of their offices - good PR opportunity, showcases UCD.	- less exposure overall than in #1 - significantly fewer prototypes can be posted than in #1. (Surprisingly, no one complained that this technique was invasive.)
3. ... in the designer's office.	- facilitates discussion between the participant and the designer - scheduled appointments for reviewing prototypes - significantly more prototypes can be posted than in either #1 or #2.	- less exposure overall than in #1 - may engender demand effects similar to those that can be present during usability testing; participants may be less inclined to give negative feedback - more labour intensive for the designer.

To this end, we are currently setting up additional asynchronous collaborative design sessions in which our home-grown list of BI experts are interacting with online prototypes, consisting of modified versions of the designs used in sessions with the extended team. During these electronic asynchronous collaborative design sessions, participants will be asked to independently review these sets of prototypes, created in PowerPoint, and provide us with feedback via the Insert > Comment function (the electronic equivalent of the sticky notes utilised in the original whiteboard versions of this design process).

After each user completes the task, the PowerPoint file, annotated with virtual sticky notes, will be returned to the designers and the prototypes will be delivered to the next participant who will receive the same instructions. As in the whiteboard exercises, these comments will contribute to the evolving foundation from which each succeeding participant will view the prototypes. Other than preparing the prototypes to be used in this way (e.g., stripping project-related details, providing a description of how the functionality is intended to be used and how it fits into the overall process of creating and maintaining an information map), we expect that this process will require limited oversight, thereby allowing us to focus on other user interface design issues during this time. We hope to find that the earlier rounds of the asynchronous design process with the extended development team will have evolved the designs beyond the more-obvious issues and so will allow the BI expert users to focus on higher-level ones.

We have also scheduled a meeting with a small group of internal customers to review the latest prototypes and gather input. This meeting will likely include aspects of both a design walk-through and a collaborative design session. Utilising the current set of prototypes as the basis for discussion, we plan initially to walk users through the designs that comprise various task flows, and to continue by inviting users to share their ideas about how those designs might be improved. In addition, users will be encouraged to communicate their design ideas by using low-fidelity materials such as markers, sticky notes and drawing paper.

In future, we plan to use additional variations on this asynchronous collaborative theme. Regardless of how we adapt the various data-gathering techniques to best fit our needs, we know that an innovative approach to design has worked well for us and has helped us make a significant contribution to many aspects of the IMS product.

SUMMARY AND CONCLUSIONS

We have found innovation and creativity essential to creating a space for usability in the actual design process, particularly when working in an environment that is not always conducive to a user-centred design process. The flexible approach described in this chapter has improved the overall usability of the IMS product in several tangible ways.

Despite the fact that no existing customer base and no pre-identified group of user-like contacts existed, we were able to create a circle of BI experts to rely on for input and information. The data gathered from the exploratory usability testing sessions with these contacts gave us the specifics we needed to begin positively affecting the basic task flow and design that were implemented before we joined the team.

We identified issues pertaining to the desirability of present and absent requirements, the suitability of features, the integration of components and the usability of the application as a whole. Follow-up usability testing confirmed that the user interface modifications that were implemented based on the initial usability data had, indeed, improved the usability of the application almost across the board.

By considering the unique needs of various members of the extended development team, we were able to communicate the usability testing results such that each team member received information relevant to their work needs, and that allowed them to move forward. Specifically, we delivered component-specific information to the components team regarding integration issues, as well as usability findings that may have affected all component-consuming products. Likewise, we met with marketing to discuss data that affected requirements. By working within the existing system for tracking bugs, we were able to help the development team prioritise issues (including those identified outside usability testing) and formulate a plan of attack for addressing them. We were also able to work with usability analysts and developers on other products, assessing the ramifications of our mutual design decisions with the goal of creating a seamless integration of the user interfaces across the BI product suite.

As we began to design for new requirements, we used the asynchronous collaborative design process to quickly detect poor design decisions and implement solutions. The asynchronous collaborative design process allowed us to quickly identify fruitless design paths, confirm whether or not our designs met the marketing requirements, and understand design deficiencies and technical limitations from people with diverse backgrounds and skill sets, including management.

The process also served as a significant communication tool within and across development teams, fostering increased component re-use, generating further exploration of requirements, and serving as a touch point between products, helping to minimise subsequent misfires. In addition, the process helped to foster a culture of usability where extended team members felt like valued contributors to the usability design process.

Perhaps as important as any other benefit of this approach, the process engendered support for the iterative nature of the design process and improved team work. Our future electronic asynchronous collaborative design sessions with our home-grown BI expert group will complete the cycle for this round of data gathering.

Ultimately, by employing a flexible array of approaches we have been able to provide more value to our product teams than would have otherwise been possible. We've simply opened our usability toolbox and combined existing tools and techniques in the ways that best met our needs.

REFERENCES

Muller, M.J., Hallewell Haslwanter, J.D., and Dayton, T. (1997). *Participatory Practices in the Software Lifecycle*. In M. Helander, T. Landauer, and Prabhu, P. (Ed.), Handbook of Human–Computer Interaction. Amsterdam: Elsevier

Muller, M.J., Tudor, L.G., Wildman, D.M., White, E.A., Root, R.W., Dayton, T., Carr, R., Diekmann, B., and Dykstra-Erickson, E.A. (1995). *Bifocal Tools for Scenarios and Representations in Participatory Activities with Users*. In J. Carroll (ed.), Scenario-Based Design For Human–Computer Interaction. New York: Wiley.

Nielsen, J. (1993) *Usability Engineering*. San Diego, CA: Academic Press.

Snyder, C. (2003) *Paper Prototyping: The Fast and Easy Way to Design and Refine User Interfaces*. New York: Morgan Kaufmann.

Tudor, L. (1995). *User-Centered Design Methodologies for an Auditory Tutorial*. In Proceedings of the Human Factors and Behavioral Sciences Symposium 1995, Holmdel, NJ: AT&T, March 1995.

Tudor, L.G., Muller, M.J., Dayton, T., and Root, R.W. (1993). *A Participatory Design Technique for High-Level Task Analysis, Critique and Redesign: The CARD Method*. In Proceedings of the Human Factors and Ergonomics Society 1993 Meeting, Seattle WA, October, 295–299.

CHAPTER 7

Changing Perceptions: Getting the Business to Value User-Centred Design Processes

Adam Polansky

This is a story about how user-centred design activities, combined with effective methods for identifying and managing client expectations, led to a successful build and launch of a website for an entertainment production company that owns several well-known venues. This two-pronged approach – technical methods combined with project-oriented methods – allowed my team to balance the needs of the business stakeholder and the intended users of the website, while permitting us to deliver on time and on budget.

Of course, projects and programmes succeed all the time. What makes this story unique? To answer that question, I'll need to tell you about the discipline of Information Architecture and something I call the Project Parameter Matrix.

WHO AM I TO TALK ABOUT THIS?

I am an information architect. What does that mean? To Rosenfeld and Morville (1998; p. 11), it means that I:

- clarify the mission and vision for a website while balancing the needs of organisation and the needs of the users;

- determine the content and functionality of the site;

- define the site's organisation, navigation, nomenclature, and search capabilities;

- design a plan for how the site will change and grow over time.

There are nearly as many definitions of information architecture as there are information architects. So let's just pick a definition and move on:

> *Information Architecture is the practice of structuring knowledge or data. These are often structured according to their context in user interactions or larger databases. The term is most commonly applied to Web development, but also applies to disciplines outside of a strict Web context, such as programming and technical writing.*

(Wikipedia, 2005)

Information Architecture, or IA, is becoming more entrenched in both small development firms and large organisations doing enterprise-level development. You'll typically find information architects (IAs) working in website development and development of Internet-connected applications. Companies who utilise IAs have figured out that in order to have a reasonable chance at launching a viable application, there should be more thought between the time that raw requirements are collected and the time that product developers begin building the application.

While the discipline of IA is still very young, the need for it is not. Businesses have always needed people who can bridge the gaps between functional areas. There are those people – I call them the 'natural liaisons' – who have always existed between camps. They bridge the gulf between groups, enable communication between them, and understand the frustrations they feel. They have a knack for bringing order to chaos. I've found that a certain intrinsic quality often brings them to the role, whatever their job title happens to be. Ask a seasoned information architect and they'll likely tell you that they were 'doing' the job before anyone knew what an IA was.

IAs are the practical application arm of the science (discipline? art? craft?) of usability. The IA incorporates the principles of usability and human–computer interaction into the documentation of a project at the outset. When the IA does their job, those principles are woven into the fabric of an application before any code is written or any testing takes place. Ideally, when formal testing is conducted on a well-designed application, the results do more to refine than redefine a project.

The relationship is not unlike that of a writer and an editor. The IAs, like writers, immerse themselves in the work, defining how an interface will function, using a combination of research and experience. Like usability engineering itself, there is as much art as science to the approach. The professionals in the usability lab have much of the same background but theirs is a more-objective view. It's not unusual to find the same person serving in both roles ... but hopefully not at the same time on the same project.

I've worked in lead roles in media development for the print, advertising, business forms and newspaper industries for over 20 years. I've been functioning as an IA for seven years – and using the title for nearly six. In this capacity, I've led projects for some of the world's largest companies, who specialise in soft drinks, office supplies, plastic bags, industrial pumps, silicon chips, entertainment, travel, consumer electronics and supply chain logistics. What I've discovered across these many and varied engagements is that, while every project has its own challenges, the sticking points are almost always the same.

THE VICIOUS CIRCLE OF DISTRUST

One of the most difficult things to accomplish on a development team is to persuade the business that there is a benefit in waiting for something. Distrust is the underlying theme to the mating dance that begins with estimates being rebuked and slashed because the business is certain that they've been wildly padded. Guess what? They *were* padded! They were padded because the development team was certain that the business owners would tell them to slash their estimate.

What else contributes to the vicious circle? I call it the 'look busy, teacher's coming' syndrome. We on the development side often succumb to the urge to actively engage everyone attached to a project at once. This results in cut corners that would make a bed-sheet look like a handkerchief that is still supposed to do the job of a bed-sheet. Why do we do this? Because it lets us show the business that we're busy, busy, busy. What happens is that the team gets started coding something … anything! And the business feels that they're spending their money wisely. After all, developers coding … that's real productivity!

So how do you persuade people who equate progress with seeing prototypes and lines of code that time spent 'thinking' will shorten time spent 'doing'? You can roll out the stock cautionary platitudes, such as 'Measure twice – cut once' or 'You never have time to do it right but you always have time to do it over.' You can apply any number of project methodologies designed to maximise the time spent planning.

Typically though, when a project really starts spooling up, the pressure to 'get working' – as opposed to planning – is relentless. The prevailing attitude in many organisations seems to be 'We know that no project plan is ever accurate, so let's just get coding.'

A WINK'S AS GOOD AS A NOD TO A BLIND MAN

There's another little dance that happens between development and businesses, and it goes something like this:

> Biz: 'Can you give me an estimation of when you'll launch?'

> Dev: 'We don't know enough yet.'

> Biz: (Cajolingly) 'I understand. Look, I just need a ballpark estimate to take to the executive committee. They know it doesn't mean anything yet. I just need to tell them something. You can make all the appropriate caveats.'

> Dev: 'Okay ... Here's a rough idea but it doesn't account for [insert unknowns here].'

Fast forward to first meeting after scope estimates are made when Dev tells Biz how long it will really take:

> Biz: 'You told me it would [pick one or more of the following]:

> (1.)   ... only cost this much!'

> (2.)   ... only take this long!'

> (3.)   ... only use this many hours!'

No one is going to go back to an executive committee to say they didn't know what they were talking about when they promised a feature set, timeline or budget. Instead, acrobatic efforts are made to wedge a project into an unreasonable set of parameters.

What gets cut? Planning. What gets delayed? Product launch.

See the connection?

Pretend for a moment that I am assigned to a web application development team. As an IA, I am responsible for shepherding the process of collecting, qualifying, organising and displaying from a functional standpoint, all the aspects of an application. I stand at the hub of communication between business stakeholders, site visitors, developers and visual designers. Ultimately, I'm the 'user advocate'. I make sure that the application is built for the site visitor first and foremost. And, I also ensure that neither the programmers nor the designers tip the balance between how something looks and how it works.

This chapter recounts the events I experienced when a business was willing to accept that, in order to meet a budget and a launch date, the project needed to be planned well – and in sufficient detail – before a single line of code was written.

THE CASE STUDY

The Client: An entertainment production company that owns several well-known venues, one of which is home to an internationally famous chorus line.

The Marketing Goal: Create a new website that distinguishes between one of the well-known venues and the production company itself, that both share the same name.

The Business Goal: Create a new website that engages visitors, lets them select an event from a calendar, get further information on that event and link to an online, commercial ticketing agency to buy their tickets.

The first items we tackled were 'due diligence' tasks. We probed the business stakeholders, attempting to discover answers to these questions:

- Who are the stakeholders?

- What is the stakeholders' vision for the new site? (And is there more than a single vision?)

- What does the current website contain?

- How does it meet (or not meet) the marketing and business goals?

- How does it meet (or not meet) the visitors' goals?

- What are visitors' perceptions of the current site?

- What features do we keep?

- What features do we lose?

- What features do we need to develop?

- What features need improvement?

- What are the technical capabilities and constraints?

And most importantly …

- What are the relative priority levels of time, cost and quality?

THE PROJECT PARAMETER MATRIX

Every project is governed by three parameters: time, cost and quality. Many projects fail because of the business owner's unwillingness to believe that these elements are intertwined with the laws of nature and cannot have equal priority. This failure mode can be avoided, however. The first step in preventing this is to establish at the outset of a project that between the three parameters:

- one has the least amount of flexibility;

- one has the greatest amount of flexibility;

- by default, something falls in the middle.

If the business and development can accomplish this, the project has a context for everything that happens after. As I mentioned above, these are laws of nature. You cannot say that more than one element is inflexible. For example: 'We have $350,000 to spend and it has to do everything Amazon.com does.' If you set those requirements, and you try to begin development, you can be as sure as the sunrise that you will have to choose between them later. Making that choice will cost you money in redevelopment and 'churn' since the decision is being made later rather than earlier.

This is the process by which my team created our project parameter matrix. In our discussions with the stakeholders, we established the following:

- Q: Between time and cost, which is least flexible? (It can be any two elements.)

  A: Cost.

- Q: Between time and quality, which is least flexible?

  A: Time.

- Q: Between cost and quality, which is least flexible?

  A: Cost.

So cost was least flexible, followed by time and quality. We displayed the relationship in a matrix (see Figure 7.1).

We knew that cost was an absolute. We had a fixed – and relatively small – budget, and we couldn't bust it. Time was an issue due to the upcoming holiday season. Quality was most flexible, which meant that we would have to look at some less-complicated or sophisticated ways of meeting the project goals.

It's important to note that quality being the most flexible element doesn't mean it isn't still critical to the project. It simply means that relatively speaking, it had more room for compromise than either cost or time.

FEATURE VALUE ANALYSIS

The next step of our engagement was to figure out exactly what features and functions we could provide, given the client's budget. It's hard to tell a customer that you can't – or won't – do everything they want. So we needed a method that would make the identification and prioritisation of features and functions a collaborative effort between us and the client.

'Feature Value Analysis' is just such a method. Feature Value Analysis is easy to perform, and best of all it puts the client in the driver's seat by allowing them to pick and choose the right mix of features and functions. In

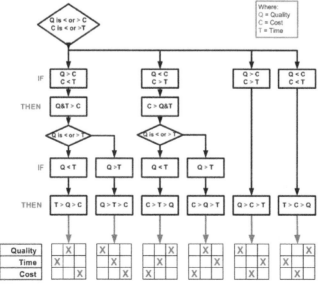

Figure 7.1   Project parameter matrix

order to perform a Feature Value Analysis for this client, we needed to do four things:

- identify the features and functions

- analyse the features and functions

- quantify the features and functions

- derive weighted scores for each function relative to the flexibility matrix.

FEATURE AND FUNCTION IDENTIFICATION

One of the products of our due diligence was an inventory of all the content and features currently on the site, as well as what was wanted or needed. We felt that this combination of existing and future content and features represented the requirements for the new site. This information can come from many places:

- business or marketing requirements documents

- brainstorm sessions

- interviews with stakeholders and site visitors

- competitive analyses

- an understanding of best practices.

FEATURE/FUNCTION ANALYSIS

In order to define the scope of a project, the requirements need to be collected and judged relative to all other requirements. The method we used is called Feature/Function Analysis. This involves making a list of all the potential features or functions that an application might contain, saying as much as you can about each one. Ideally this includes a description of the features, estimates of their value to a site visitor and the business, as well as the ease of implementation. Additional information can be captured as well, such as the 'content owner', dependencies on or features provided by an external vendor, the name of the system that currently supports the content, and whether the feature is specific to a particular internal business unit. Anything that helps the team characterise each feature or function is fair game for the Feature/Function Analysis.

QUANTIFYING THE LIST

It's fairly common to look at a list like this and ask the business to rate each of the items on some kind of 1 to 5 scale as to their level of importance to the application. While that provides some way to differentiate the 'must-haves' from the 'nice-to-haves', it still doesn't take into consideration the project parameters. And it's subject to the whims of the person or persons doing the rating.

In this project, one team member was absolutely certain that there needed to be an 'interactive paper doll' of one of the chorus-line dancers. Almost everyone could immediately see that this particular feature didn't really support the goals of the business or the visitors. And it would have been rather costly to implement. But this particular team member was not someone who could be directly rebuffed. So paper dolls made the list. How could we get to the conclusion we knew was appropriate without risking our jobs or the contract? The process we used is called Contextual Qualification.

CONTEXTUAL QUALIFICATION

Every feature or function on the Feature/Function Analysis list can be characterised according to three criteria:

- value to the business

- value to the site visitors

- ease of implementation.

To determine a feature's value to the business, we asked the business stakeholders to rate each feature's ability to meet business goals on a 1 to 5 scale, with 1 indicating low ability and 5 indicating high ability. We computed value to site visitors by asking visitors to the site to rate each feature's ability to help them achieve their goals – whatever they happened to be – upon entering the site. Finally, we gauged ease of implementation by asking our technical team to rate each feature using the same 1 to 5 scale.

In this way, every feature and function was scrutinised from three separate perspectives. The next step was to weight the scores based on the project parameter matrix. During this step, we made the following assumptions:

- cost can be mapped to business value

- time can be mapped to ease of implementation

- quality can be mapped to site visitor value.

Remember that we had already established that cost was least flexible. To reflect this, we multiplied the business value ratings by 3. Time was the next most critical parameter, so we multiplied ease of implementation ratings by 2. Since quality was most flexible, we did not transform the visitor value ratings.

The weighted scores for each feature were summed and divided by 3, yielding a weighted value for each feature. The feature list was then ordered from high to low to create a relative priority level among the features. The obvious needs landed at the top of the list while the questionable ones (read: paper dolls) fell to the bottom.

For the purposes of this project, estimates were made by the development team of the number of hours each feature would require. Those hours were multiplied by a reference hourly rate. The product of these two numbers represented the amount of money it would take to implement every single feature.

We knew exactly how much the client was spending on the project, so we proceeded down the feature list, adding up cost points until we reached the budget threshold. A line was drawn as a cut-off and we reviewed everything above and below the line to see if the features above the cut-off constituted a complete solution. Then we took the list back to the client.

HORSE TRADING

With the feature list rank-ordered and qualified, we sat down with the client. We made it clear that the point of this exercise was to review the features above the cut-off and propose the scope of the project from that list. We would also review the list below the cut-off to make sure that nothing was being dismissed out of hand.

We then offered the client the opportunity to 'horse trade'. If they wanted to move something from the bottom of the list to the top, they could. They would have to sacrifice something of equal or greater point value from the top. We also made it clear that we were not there to negotiate price.

So we haggled. For the most part the client agreed that we had scoped a complete solution and they were willing to trade some of the 'low-hanging fruit'. The end result was that the client was satisfied with the scope of the project because they were able to make informed decisions about each feature relative to the whole project. They knew what was in and why. They knew what was out and why. They made the decisions themselves, rather than taking our word that we knew what we were doing.

The tangible advantage of Feature Value Analysis is that by taking a faceted approach to evaluating each feature, you can identify the obvious winners. At the same time, you bring the obvious 'dogs' into sharp relief, thus eliminating them from negotiation without pitting personal preferences against each other. This allows the team to sort out the greyer areas, on the basis of more than a subjective whim.

SITE MAPS

There are as many formats for site maps as there are professionals who create them. One is pretty much as good as another, as long as it conveys the relationship of a page or content area to the site at large. From my perspective,

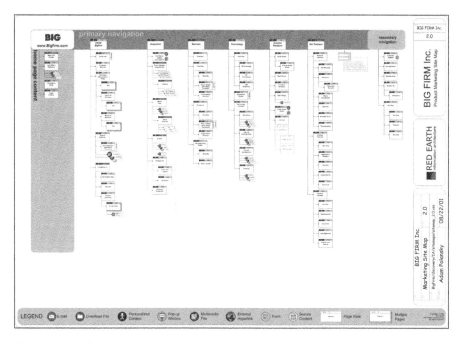

Figure 7.2   Site map

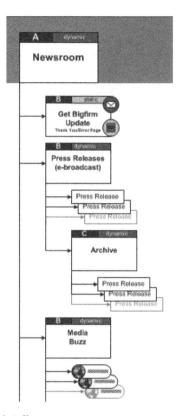

Figure 7.3   Site map detail

I found that a site map could fulfil more than this basic requirement by incorporating a certain amount of metadata.[1] In the course of Feature Value Analysis we determined a number of things that characterised each element within the site:

- static versus data-driven content

- third-party content

- downloadable files and their types (for example, .pdf)

- information strata – where a page lies within a hierarchy.

This approach helps make a site map a more-valuable working document. It characterises information, rather than just linking it together.

---

1   Metadata has come to be used to refer to data about data. A good example is a library catalogue card, which contains data about the nature and location of the data in the book referred to by the card. (Free-Definition: www.free-definition.com/Metadata.html).

'AS-IS', 'TO BE' AND 'TO BE LATER'

We had the scope defined. We knew exactly what we were building and what it would consist of in terms of content. What we had to do next was organise it. We proceeded by defining the site in three different ways:

- how it was today

- how it would be when we finished the project

- how it should be after the next project was complete.

The site map was then constructed using icons, each containing a collection of information relevant to the page or content area it represented.

'AS-IS'

Before attempting to make wholesale changes to the organisation of the site, I chose to map the site as it was. What surfaced was the fact that certain events produced by the client had their own mini-sites, often with a different look and feel. Some of these mini-sites used very little of the client's branding. We could see at a glance that the client's main content was sparse to non-existent.

We decided to create templates for event-specific mini-sites that would showcase an event within the client's brand identity. We also decided to make more content available within the site proper, rather than pushing the visitors off to other sites via hyperlink.

'TO BE'

Using the feature list, I created icons for each item that had made the cut for the first phase of development and used them as the building blocks of the site map. The map performed three functions:

- it provided a structured look at each content segment;

- it indicated global or resident content that would be present throughout the site;

- it highlighted time-sensitive or featured content that would be available from the home page.

'TO BE LATER'

Items that weren't completely abandoned but slated for 'future development' were incorporated into a copy of the 'To Be' map, with 'to be' items in colour and 'to be later' items in greyscale. This became a budget projection tool for the business.

WIREFRAMES

Before computers and the Internet generated new meanings for old terms, a 'thumbnail sketch' was a quick, pencil rendering of how an advertisement might look. It was typically done on a layout pad and its only function was to 'try on' an idea in some kind of rough format before committing to a particular direction.

Wireframes serve the same function. They are rough models that represent how content on a page can be organised.

Since they are usually developed in applications like Visio, Omnigraffle or Photoshop, they can be sophisticated to the point that they look and even act

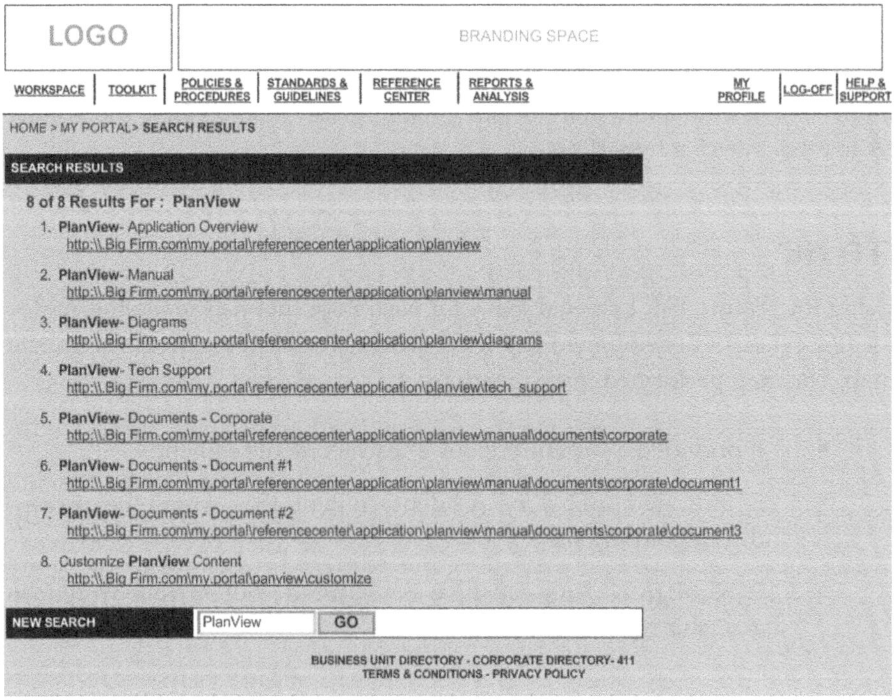

Figure 7.4   An example of a wireframe

like a finished website. Putting that much effort into wireframes defeats their true purpose. One of the most immutable laws of nature is that 'form follows function'. This is true whether you're a chef preparing a meal or a molecular biologist puzzling out the next generation of medications for cancer. While it may seem that you're saving steps by locking down the design, you are actually creating a bias toward a page layout based on its appearance rather than its function.

By modelling pages around their function without visual design elements or colour palettes, you have the freedom to move things on, off or around the page based exclusively on the merits of their functionality and without feeling restricted by a design scheme. If you let the visual design dictate how a page works, you're letting the tail wag the dog.

The key thing to remember about wireframes is that they are working documents. They should be rearranged, marked up, crossed out and written over. This is the time to begin talking to the back-end developers to make sure that what you're proposing on the screen will be supported by the system. Wireframes give you the vehicle for testing and validating concepts and revising the interface, while the cost is negligible.

BUILT-IN FUNCTIONALITY

With this particular client, we had only two charters: distinguish the production company from the venues, and create a calendar to help users find and learn about an event before they were taken to a third party to purchase their tickets.

In this case the wireframes were fairly homogeneous. We needed to represent a home page, we needed to represent sub-pages for each segment or 'A-level page' on the site and all internal or 'B-level pages'.

The brand effort was managed within the presentation layer by introducing the client at the home page and by displaying events in a way that was agnostic about their venues. Venues themselves were relegated to one particular section of the site where the user could learn all they wanted about the history of the venue, or logistical information such as parking or services for the disabled.

Events were located in the calendar and once again they were presented in a way that was not specific to a venue. Users could see a calendar of all events within a particular time frame and/or filter the calendar by selecting particular event types such as 'Theatricals', 'Comedy' or 'Family Shows'. The calendar would refresh itself with only those events that fell within the specified categories.

To help clients make a decision about an event, we used the wireframes as the prototype to prove the back-end functionality of the site. The development team created a working model of the site, using the wireframe as the interface. When we went into the usability lab, we had a working prototype to support the test without having invested ourselves too deeply in a design style.

The recommendations that came from testing were primarily cosmetic, meaning that any issues could be remedied by emphasising or de-emphasising attributes on the page, changing labels or simply re-ordering parts of a task. These recommendations served to inform the design team as they created the final face of the site.

In the case of this particular site, formal testing yielded no systemic recommendations. In lieu of saying, 'They lived happily ever after', however, I can report that the site made its launch window, stayed within budget and remained in place for nearly four years. In fact, even though the site has been through several visual design updates, the structure defined by our work remains.

WHY A SUCCESS?

It has always been difficult to convey the value of Information Architecture to someone who has not been exposed to it in a project environment. To many people, if you can't point to an amount of money, the benefits sound abstract.

Can I say: 'You'll save this much money by incorporating a User-Centred Design process'? No.

At best, all I can say is 'Remember how much money, time or functionality you lost on the last (if not every) project you sponsored? Well, I can definitely reduce if not eliminate that.'

Believe it or not, this doesn't send prospective clients looking for their chequebooks.

Someone who considers programming to be 'real' work is likely to think Information Architecture and the processes are 'navel-gazing' obstacles to production. Product managers and other business stakeholders are notoriously impatient and an extended cycle of planning doesn't yield the kinds of working examples in the time frame that they're used to seeing them in.

It is certainly possible to create a working prototype from a set of raw requirements, or to come up with a beautiful look and feel from that same source. However, it's the time spent to sync them up and the effort that goes into re-programming to support undefined business rules or unproven functionality that sit at the end of the project, eat up your money, make you miss your launch and result in a sub-standard product.

To paraphrase a quote given to me by an associate 'A week of programming will save you an hour of planning.'

REFERENCES

Rosenfeld, L., and Morville, P. (1998). *Information Architecture for the World Wide Web*. Sebastopol, CA: O'Reilly.

Wikipedia. (2005). *Information Architecture*. Retrieved from http://en.wikipedia. org/wiki/Information_architecture, December 2005.

CHAPTER 8

User Interface (UI) Design at Siemens Medical Solutions

Dirk Zimmermann and Jean Anderson

Over the last four years the Health Services Division of Siemens Medical Solutions have been implementing a user-centred design process into their product management and development organisations for their new flagship product. Bringing a strong user focus into a large organisation has to be done under certain constraints and requires adaptation of known processes to the specific organisational needs and realities.

This case study outlines the application domain, the organisational structure and the detailed process that has been established. It also describes the introduction strategy together with the obstacles and facilitators.

WHO WE ARE AND WHAT WE DO

Siemens Medical Solutions, a unit of Siemens AG, is one of the largest suppliers to the healthcare industry. The company is known for bringing together innovative medical technologies, healthcare information systems and management consulting and support services, to help customers achieve tangible and sustainable clinical and financial outcomes. From imaging systems for diagnosis, to therapy equipment for treatment, to patient monitors to hearing instruments and beyond, Siemens innovations contribute to the health and well-being of people across the globe, while improving operational efficiencies and optimising workflow in hospitals, clinics, home health agencies and doctors' offices.

The Health Services Division of Siemens Medical Solutions USA produces software applications for the healthcare industry. Our products run the gamut of clinical, financial and administrative applications. We both work on the newer web-based clinical applications. Although web-based, they are complex, flexible and feature-rich applications designed for use by doctors, nurses and other medical staff in recording, planning and tracking patient care.

The management team for the suite of clinical products that we work on has made a very strong commitment to incorporate UI design early on within our product development methodology. They have consistently supported us in the effort to improve UI design practices across all the company's software products. (Although we work on the clinical products and our case study will focus on our experiences there, there are other teams replicating our efforts in the financial and administrative applications.)

This commitment is reflected in the marketing campaign for our products, where the concept of a 'smart UI' is featured as one of the top three selling points. This selling point has become a mission statement for our team of UI designers.

We define a smart UI as one that doesn't seem to be there at all – it gives the end-users what they need, when they need it, so that they can recognise it and use it without barriers.

How were we lucky enough to get senior management to make such a commitment? It was largely due to the success experienced several years ago by the Medical Solutions Hardware Division. There, a major effort was implemented to redesign the UIs of the medical devices so that they were consistent with each other and consistently user-friendly. The redesign was successful and helped positively affect sales of those products. We are now trying to build on that success in the software arena.

STRUCTURE OF OUR PRODUCT TEAM

Each application in our application suite is conceived and created by a product team. Our product teams split the phases of the classic product development cycle into two main chunks (see Figure 8.1).

The product management team is responsible for the product vision, the requirements and the UI design. The results of its work are then turned over to the development team, which is responsible for building, testing and supporting the product. Since the product management team is where we UI designers 'live', that's the part of the development cycle we'll focus on in this case study.

A typical product management team consists of a product manager, between five and twelve product analysts, a UI designer and a systems analyst.

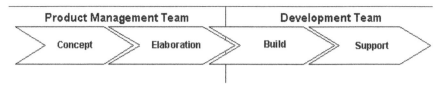

Figure 8.1   The product development cycle at Siemens Medical Solutions

The product manager is an expert in each product's market area, is responsible for soliciting high-level requirements, for guiding the product vision and producing the market requirements specification document, or MRD.

The product analysts are experts in the medical domain of the product. They have prior experience practising medicine. They maintain current licensing and certification for their medical skills. (Some continue to practise on a part-time basis.) They are responsible for the functional requirements, user analysis and workflow analysis. They produce two major artefacts: the user profile and the detailed use cases which are derived from the user profile.

The UI designers are experts in interaction design and/or usability engineering. They are responsible for defining the usability requirements, creating interaction designs and validating the user interface and interaction designs. They produce the user interface specifications.

The systems analysts are experts in object-oriented analysis and/or database architecture. They are responsible for authoring the technical requirements of the system, as well as creating the object-oriented modelling for a system's components and data structures.

Achieving consistency in the user interfaces of multiple products is very challenging when each UI designer works alone with a product team. We needed a way to foster among the UI designers the creative collaboration that lets design standards evolve naturally from the design work and encourages adherence to those standards. Consequently, while each product management team has a UI designer assigned to it, all the UI designers actually belong to a separate UI team.

This structure allows the UI designers to work together in sharing design ideas across products, evolving the user interface standards, checking each other for consistency and mentoring new team members. Our team of UI designers currently has eleven members and provides UI designs for eight software products.

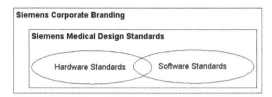

Figure 8.2   Layers of standards

Not all the members of the UI team are assigned to product teams. There are a number of topics or concepts that apply to all the clinical products. For example, the concept of an electronic patient chart that allows a doctor, nurse or nurse-practitioner to browse through the patient's medical history is a universal concept in all our clinical products. There is a UI designer assigned to that concept. Whenever a product team needs to enhance a universal concept, such as the patient's history, the UI designer assigned to that concept works with the UI designer assigned to the product team. Instant design buddies! A UI designer rarely works alone in this structure.

The UI team is also supported by a group of visual designers who operate at the level of corporate branding and are responsible for the over arching style guide that applies to all Siemens products. They work as consultants within each general product area, reviewing layouts and icons for visual consistency.

The need for these internal consultants stems from our goal of finding/developing commonalities in the UI designs of our clinical software applications and our medical hardware. More and more frequently, our end-users expect to use both as part of their day-to-day work. They also expect the hardware and software products to interact seamlessly.

From a standards perspective this means that we have several layers of design standards to follow in order to support the company's branding strategy and create consistency among the various medical hardware and software products that interact within the end-user's environment.

EXPLORING THE MEDICAL DOMAIN, OR WHY WE LEAVE USER ANALYSIS TO THE PRODUCT ANALYSTS

Designing user interfaces for software in the medical domain presents some unique benefits and challenges that have pushed us to modify our design process from the more 'typical' user-centred design methodologies.

Among the benefits of working in the medical domain is the fact that we can rely on all the end-users having had medical training. This means that they have all had college-level or higher education. They also share a large body of clinical knowledge that is completely separate from their experience with computers. As a result, some UI elements such as terminology require less focus. Within most areas of medicine, these end-users have an established and known lexicon. Indeed, many things hardly need labelling. When looking at a list of data values labelled 'vital signs', for example, any doctor can tell the patient's weight from their blood pressure, just by looking at the data.

Design validations are also amazingly easy in this domain! Doctors, especially, show a very high level of confidence in their knowledge of their work and can be counted on to react critically when a system is not designed to match their mental models. Nurses will demonstrate a similar level of self-confidence, especially if you've managed to get the doctors out of the room. These are not the type of end-users who will assume a problem is due to their own error or who will be timid about voicing their opinions.

> *Since coming to the medical product domain a little over a year ago, I have changed my approach to design validations. Nowadays, I always ask to have two to three people who perform the same role together in a single session. In this arena, that will guarantee you a good deal of argument and discussion as the users voice their varied opinions of the information presentation and the interaction.*
>
> *These discussions are wonderfully enlightening and always provide new insights on the users' mental models. Of course, I've been lucky in that the users I've worked with somehow manage to reach a consensus by the end of the session. I know some of my colleagues have not been so fortunate.*
>
> (Jean Anderson)

These days, clinicians also have experience in using computers – again thanks to their higher education and to the increasing use of advanced technology in medicine. As little as five years ago, doctors over 50 years old didn't want to use computers and often made their nurses and residents do the computer work for them. Today, doctors of all ages (including the 50+ group) carry PDAs and always ask us when they will be able to synchronise appointment schedules and clinical patient data between the PDAs and our products.

In addition, medical personnel have very strong mental models of the clinical tasks that they routinely perform. When you can get them away from their patients, they are able to discuss their clinical tasks and decision-making processes in abstract or in great detail. They can separate themselves from the current reality of how they do 'X' now and focus on the question of what's the best way to do 'X'. Many of them are accustomed to discussing best practices as they participate in defining or refining the policies and practices within the institution where they work.

It's not all easy, however. Among the challenges of designing for medical end-users is the fact that contextual inquiry is of limited value in this domain unless the UI designers happen to have medical degrees as well. Medical staff, and especially doctors, are trained to make clinical decisions rapidly and often can't take the time to explain their decisions while on the job. And because we do not want to interfere with patient care, there are no opportunities while observing a doctor at work to interrupt and inquire what happened in that last five seconds while the doctor looked over a patient chart.

> *My first experience in observing chart rounds in an oncology department was definitely an eye-opener. I was very used to using contextual inquiry from my work on other non-medical software products and very pleased when the clinical product team agreed that I should do some field observations to understand the work environment of our clinical end-users. Thanks to Hollywood, most of us are familiar with scenes of doctors walking through a hospital, making their 'rounds' and visiting patients while accompanied by various medical residents and interns.*

> *In outpatient care, it's a little different. The medical team gathers in a meeting room to discuss their current cases. As I sat in the back of the room and tried to observe, the medical team got through almost half a dozen cases before I even grasped the rhythm of their review process. It was amazing – a team of about ten doctors, nurses and therapists sitting round a table.*

> *Each case was introduced by stating the patient's age, gender and diagnosis, and displaying a recent film (X-ray or CT scan.) The team would look at an image and every one of them saw what issues needed to be discussed while I was still trying to figure out what it was a picture of.*

> *I must have looked as baffled as I felt because our doctor–host and the product analyst with me began whispering explanations in my ear to*

help me follow the discussions. A dozen more cases flew by before I could follow the team's discussions enough to capture observations on the type of data referenced for each case, the interactions within the team and the communication flows between the team's members.

Subsequent field studies to observe nursing and other medical staff in their work environments produced similar results – it is extraordinarily difficult to follow these end-users without another medical person there to explain. You can't interrupt the clinician under observation – that would interfere with patient care. So you need an 'interpreter' to explain the decisions being made or considered and provide general medical background.

(Jean Anderson)

It can also be challenging to find medical staff who are willing to participate in product design. Patient care is a demanding field of work. The doctors, nurses and therapists who use our products have made an enormous commitment to their work and to their patients. They've been through years of training. They put in long hours on a regular basis. Then along we come, asking them to spend time away from their patients to help us design a better product. They may want better tools to use, but they went to medical school because they wanted to help people.

The clinician's initial response to the idea of participating in the product design is typical – it's flattering, it's exciting. They're pleased to be asked. It makes sense to them that they should participate. But that response only goes so far. If we can't show them the tangible results of their input, they lose interest. If we ask for too much of their time, they get annoyed – it's time away from patients. After all, their commitment is to their patients and that's where their hearts are. Having better tools to use would be nice, but most doctors have lived in the world of paper records and know they can get along quite well without a PC.

Our solution to these challenges is a product management team consisting of medical experts and design experts and a process that supports close collaboration between the two.

OUR PROCESS

Since we work as part of the product management team, our process focuses on the concept and elaboration phases of the overall product development cycle.

CONCEPT PHASE

During the concept phase, the product analysts – as the medical domain experts – write detailed profiles of the targeted end-users. This artefact is primarily for the use of the UI designers and its template was actually created by a joint team of product analysts and UI designers so that we could be sure it would contain the user analysis we need.

Ideally, a user profile contains the following sections:

- Training and certification required for the role.

- Specialties that may cause variations in the role.

- Nature of the relationship with patients.

- How would this person define their primary responsibility in this role?

- What obstacles/challenges does a person in this role face?

- What makes a person feel secure/insecure in this role?

- Demographics of the average users in this role:

  - gender and age

  - experience level with PCs

  - length of time a person spends in this role

  - other roles a person may fill concurrently.

- Description of the work environment:

  - outpatient or inpatient care

  - physical environments (types of exam rooms, treatment rooms, offices for patient consultation, for research, etc.).

- Organisational chart – who does this person report to, who reports to them?

  - roles this person interacts with.

- Typical workload and schedule.

- Tasks performed by a person in this role, and for each task:

  - triggers

- preconditions

- task analysis

- post conditions.

Once a user profile is completed, the product analyst begins to plan which of the user's tasks will be features in the product and which users perform those tasks, and to compile a grid of use cases (tasks or sub-tasks) and user-actors where detailed analysis is needed.

At the same time, the UI analyst categorises the tasks from the user profiles, by plotting them on the matrix in Figure 8.3.

This model – partly based on the Action–Regulation Theory by Hacker (1994) – differentiates between two levels of action regulation. The first one is the action-planning level, where users coordinate their different (sub-) tasks and set goals for their next (inter-) actions. Tasks on this level are, for example, work lists that group actions by type and allow users to quickly assess how much work needs to be done for a given task type, or a patient list that indicates patients' current clinical condition in order to direct users' focus to the relevant data or information area.

The second one is the action-execution level, where users actually perform a clinical task, such as review medical records, document a patient's condition

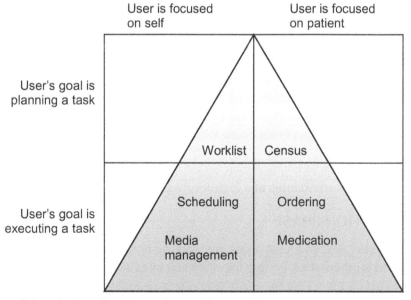

Figure 8.3   Action-planning and execution matrix.

or enter an order. Tasks on this level are usually grouped by elements on the planning level, which provides the entry point and control centre for any work a clinician is supposed to perform with the system. There are usually more execution-level tasks than planning tasks in a clinical world, so the planning area of the system – even though it is the central entry point into most workflows – is a smaller part of the overall system.

Additionally, the model differentiates between tasks that belong together because of the mere fact that the current user has to perform them, and tasks that belong together because they pertain to the same patient. This distinction is very important in the clinical world, where a holistic patient view needs to be available in any medical decision process, but where there is also a multitude of administrative tasks in which the complete patient context would inhibit rather than facilitate efficient task completion. An example to distinguish these is the prescription of a drug (patient focus is essential to avoid adverse reactions) versus the documentation of material utilised in the operating theatre over a day.

From this we can determine roughly where in an existing product a new feature or workflow will fit, predict whether we'll need new UIs or be able to re-use and enhance existing ones. And we develop a high-level navigation model indicating approximately how the user will access the feature/workflow and how it fits within the product as a whole.

The next step is to map the planned use cases to the planned UIs so that we can organise the work in 'packages' of related requirements. One of the challenges we usually face when working with a new product management team at this point is getting the systems analysts to accept that there usually isn't a one-to-one relationship between use cases and UIs. Our solution to this is to create a grid that cross-refers the user tasks from the user profiles to the relevant use case(s) and user interfaces planned. This tool allows the analysts and developers to look up which artefacts they need for each work package.

Figure 8.4 is an example of a high-level navigation model.

ELABORATION PHASE

In this phase, the product analysts are working on the use cases while the UI designers work on the UIs. Together they validate their work with actual end-users.

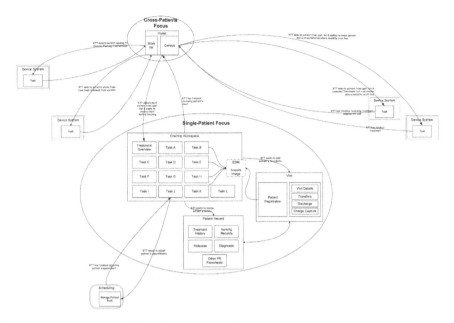

Figure 8.4   A sample high-level navigation model

One of the rules or guidelines we've had to establish is that the use case cannot in any way describe the UI. While this rule helps draw the line between the functional requirements of 'what does this thing do' and the non-functional requirements of 'how that is presented to the user', it has also been one of the challenges in propagating our process across the various product teams. Almost all the product and system analysts, in our experience, start visualising the UI long before the UI designer starts sketching the layouts.

In the simpler cases, we can work with them on re-wording the use case to avoid describing a potential UI layout ('Please don't say that she clicks a button to do 'X', just say the user chooses to do 'X.') In the tougher cases, where the product analyst has very strong opinions about the UI layout, we've had to mock up the UIs both ways and ask the users to indicate which way is better. In recent memory, the users have always either voted for our layout or given us insights that led to joint development of a third and better design.

During this phase, close collaboration between the product analysts and the UI designer is the key to success. To emphasise and build in support for this, we developed a process which we affectionately call the 'Seven Steps to UI Happiness' (see Figure 8.5).

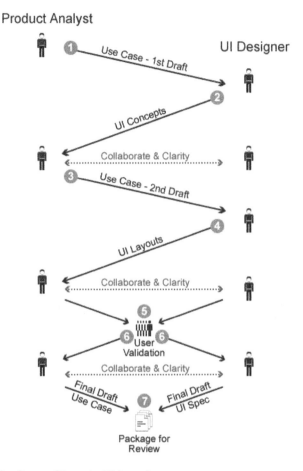

Figure 8.5   The Seven Steps to UI happiness

Step 1: The product analyst writes the first draft of the use case's main flow and sends it to the UI designer

For many product analysts, this step has been one of the hardest to get used to. They tend to be very shy of showing draft documents. In many cases, the UI designers have had to survive myriad warnings of 'it's just a draft'; 'it's not really stable yet' until the analyst learned to trust that our role at this stage is to provide a visual representation of their analysis, and not necessarily to critique their analysis.

Step 2: The UI designer produces concept and interaction diagrams and sends them to the product analyst

This is another step that product analysts have to adjust to if they're not used to working with us. Many of them are mentally visualising a UI (as they would design it) while they write the use case. So they expect UI layouts immediately and are startled by concept diagrams.

The reason for emphasising this step is that the UI designer is often learning new material about the medical domain at this stage. The diagrams allow the UI designer and product analyst to focus on the concepts involved in a task without getting entangled in discussions about details, such as wording of field labels or the use of radio buttons versus combo-boxes.

Figure 8.6 provides an example of an interaction diagram.

The hidden (to the product analysts) advantage of this step is that the concept and interaction diagrams often expose patterns of interaction. Diagrams in hand, the UI designer can discuss the patterns with other UI designers and compare notes with those who have used the pattern before.

On our team, it is very typical for a UI designer to call a 'creative' meeting at this stage. We pull in the UI designers from products that might have something similar, discuss the concepts and the interactions involved, and determine whether our interaction diagram appears to be a pattern, whether the new UI can 'borrow' effectively from an earlier one and whether the pattern should 'graduate' to a standard.

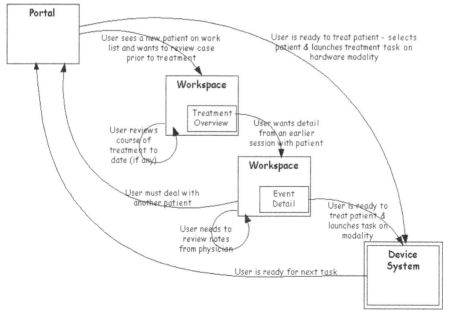

Figure 8.6   An interaction diagram involving integrated use of a web application and a medical device

Step 3: The product analyst expands the use case with alternative flows as needed and sends the new draft to the UI designer

This is a typical step in object-oriented analysis – working through the variations of the task. One advantage to having medical experts write the use cases is that they can more easily limit the alternative flows to those that are clinically reasonable.

We've found that the system designers can invent an almost infinite number of alternative flows, but the medical expert can rule out a large number of variations on the basis of 'no doctor/nurse/therapist in his right mind would do that'. The medical expert can also easily identify any variations that need to be prevented in order to avoid compromising patient safety.

Step 4: The UI designer derives the types of UIs needed (screens versus dialogues, for example) from the concepts and produces rough sketches of all the UIs needed for the use case

Obviously, these two steps get repeated as often as needed. At this stage, the UI designer is generally relying on the product analyst to draw from their clinical experience and represent the targeted user as they work together through however-many design iterations are needed to reach a stable UI layout that's worth taking out to end-users outside the company. Together they may also pull in medical experts from related product areas to cross-check their thinking.

Step 5: The design is validated with users

Once the use case flows and the UI layouts are stable, the product analyst and UI designer invent a patient and a case and create a storyboard of the task flow, showing how a user would perform the task. The storyboard is taken to hospitals where the appropriate medical staff have agreed to participate in our product design work.

This is the step that gets the most variation across the various product teams. On the team where Jean works, rather than scheduling validation sessions for each use case and UI package, they developed a schedule of monthly clusters of small validation sessions over the course of the elaboration phase. ('Small' meaning two to three users in a session that lasts about two hours. A cluster would include two to four such sessions.) This allowed the team to carry out some iterative work on the more-complex use cases, while validating the design work of the simpler ones. This schedule also made it easier to track which users had been shown what, so that we could be sure not to revisit a particular doctor before we'd had a chance to incorporate their feedback into the design.

Other product teams have preferred to hold off on design validations until all the use cases and UIs are more or less complete. They then hold large validation sessions that cover the product release as a whole. In some cases, this is a matter of cost-efficiency. For example, when your users are in Europe, monthly trips for validation would be nice but extremely expensive!

Step 6: The product analyst and UI designer review the input from the validation session(s), decide what needs to be incorporated right away, and update the UI design and use case as needed

Step 7: The final drafts of the UI spec and use cases are sent for review by the full product management team and the lead system designers from the development team

In our company's quality management programme, the system designers and other stakeholders must approve these artefacts before the project can proceed to the Build phase.

One of the primary advantages of this process is that it produces a set of milestones that a project manager can use to track the product management team's progress through the Elaboration phase. In addition, our UI team has been able to put average effort estimates on the UI steps that can be used to generate a basic project plan and schedule as soon as the team has agreed on the use cases to be worked on.

Among the seven steps are interim points labelled 'collaborate and clarify'. These represent points where the product analyst and UI designer naturally start 'sync'ing up' their work. Since these occur naturally, they are difficult to track on a project schedule (sometimes we do them without noticing!). We've found it more efficient to use just the seven steps as the milestones for tracking progress, but we include the interim points in the diagram to emphasise the collaboration – especially when we're introducing the process to a new product management team.

Finally, at the end of the Elaboration phase, a final, general review of all the work packages is held. This is an intensive period when representatives of all the internal stakeholders (documentation, testing, development etc.) are present to ask questions and provide feedback while the product analysts and UI designers present their work.

HOW WE GOT THERE

At the point in time when an organisation decides to implement a user-centred design process, they are usually already performing some of the required tasks in one way or another – not necessarily by the book or in any recommended form, but one can usually find at least some kind of requirements analysis and engineering, some form of system conceptualisation and some forms of user/customer validation in the existing processes.

While these have been implemented in a less-structured and methodological way, it's important to consider these existing efforts when planning new/additional ones and re-distributing tasks to different or additional roles.

When we started implementing a new user-centred approach to product analysis and design, we were faced with a situation that carried several challenges.

The first was that there was no dedicated UI design team. The company had an infant, centralised usability engineering team and a usability lab for validation, but their progress in educating the product development teams and convincing them to include usability engineering in their processes had been slow and frustrating. What success they had was in getting product teams to add a phase for usability testing just prior to the product's beta test, rather than to convince them of the need to incorporate better design practices up front.

A second challenge was that the company had been undergoing a merger. We were faced with five different clinical project teams working on solutions in pretty much the same domain, but of course each was using a different underlying technology, as well as a different approach to conceptualising their individual systems.

Prior to the merger, these project teams belonged to different companies (not to mention that they were located in four different countries) and there was no overarching framework or style guide that could have kept these efforts aligned, and all of these projects were already in the middle of their analysis work. Yet their work needed to be merged into a single product solution to reduce redundant efforts within the new, merged, company structure.

When examining the processes of the various projects closely, we found that user interface design actually wasn't even a defined task during any of the systems analysis and design methodologies in use. In general, requirements were being gathered as singular, unrelated elements (and had no workflow context set around them).

These two factors meant that the product analysts were faced with the request to provide some framework specification of how the system is supposed to fulfil the long list of feature requirements. In order to do this, the product analysts included sketches, example screens from other systems or their own mock-up screens to illustrate the concept of the desired functionality – expecting the technical designers and developers to translate these into consistent screens.

On the development side, however, the sketches were often enough taken verbatim and coded exactly as shown by the product analysts' artefact, even though they were labelled as illustrations or examples. Both sides expected the other party to come up with the actual UI design, a situation that is not uncommon in a lot of traditional development processes.

GOAL AND EXPECTED OUTCOME OF OUR PROCESS REDESIGN

When we started implementing a more user-centred process, the initial question was whether the process redesign and its roll-out to the product teams was supposed to be evolutionary or revolutionary. Looking at the existing common practices, it was obvious that there were multiple shortcomings that needed to be addressed, covering almost every role in the Product Management Division. Consequently, from that perspective, the revolutionary approach seemed reasonable.

However, the several different processes in place had already gathered a substantial amount of analysis knowledge in various formats, and it would be a lot of work to redo this effort in a more user-focused way. This spoke more to the evolutionary approach of slowly migrating parts of the projects/packages to a new model.

> The question of 'evolution versus revolution' in process redesign is frequently posed. For every new project, product or release, an organisation should evaluate whether an optimised process could improve their performance in meeting the company's business goals (e.g. decrease time-to-market, increase usability and decrease requirement volatility). No one wants to make the same mistakes more than once.

However, the value of stable and predictable processes shouldn't be underestimated. The key stakeholders (product analysts, UI designers and system designers) gather experience and skills and any new process requires re-training or brings along other process losses. For example, if the method of writing/managing documentation is changed, there is also a risk of needing to re-do at least part of the already existing documentation, which is generally not productive work.

In our experience, the deciding factor came to be the degree of innovation or independence from existing solutions. For example, when we consider a new release of an existing product, it's usually not worth completely changing the process model, so an evolution in smaller steps is more appropriate. On the other hand, for the new generation of a product, revolutionising the process is appropriate in order to set it up correctly from the beginning.

(Dirk Zimmermann)

Both options had pros and cons, so the deciding factor had to be on a different level in order for the decision to be acceptable throughout the whole organisation. In our case, this was achieved through a joint technology and marketing effort. Siemens announced that the upcoming clinical solution would be web-based and would provide a smart, workflow-driven and integrated user interface. This management decision was easily translated into product and process requirements: new technology/architecture constraints require revisiting the existing analysis, a workflow and integration focus requires a different view on the configuration of features, and a smart UI requires the task of UI design to exist in the analysis and design process.

There were several key goals for the new analysis and design process. The first one was to ensure that we had proper user and task analysis throughout the analysis phases and sufficient stakeholder and user validation to complement and confirm the analysis work. The second one was to define a consistent UI design framework as a basis for all upcoming products within the new family of products.

There were of course other organisational goals we needed to meet, such as conformance with the organisation's development processes, generating testable requirements and ensuring adequate attention to internationalisation issues.

INTRODUCING THE NEW PROCESS

Before the introduction of the actual analysis process we set up a pilot phase, where an interdisciplinary team of clinicians, analysts and UI designers developed the first vision demo for the new application. We invited key individuals to participate in our effort and accelerate the concept work, based on the individuals' previous experience.

During this thee-week effort we piloted all aspects of user-centred design (workflow/context analysis, UI conceptualisation, validation, visual design etc.) and managed to prototype a high-level storyboard to show the screen layouts and the new approach to system conceptualisation.

Based on the results of this pilot phase, we were able to obtain buy-in from management and the various process and project stakeholders for our process, and the approval to move ahead with this approach and plan the process implementation – and how to propagate it across the product teams. Having a compelling goal/vision for the whole organisation to see facilitated the subsequent tasks and provided an effective means for explaining the required changes to all stakeholders.

The introduction of the process happened on several levels. The first level was adapting and optimising a requirements analysis process based on use cases. The designated role for this task was the product analyst, but since a good part of the use case audience was the UI designer, there was a lot of initial collaboration to focus the artefact on the right elements and levels of detail. In several projects, this was done through a pilot package, where product analysts and UI designers collaborated on a small work package, both for education and – as an added bonus – for project planning and effort estimation reasons.

The outcome of this use case-based analysis was not only continued conformance with the existing processes, but also the conveyance of much more clinical knowledge than stand-alone requirements. The use case documents allowed the subject matter experts to share their knowledge and experience with the downstream organisation in a coordinated and effective way.

During the collaboration on use cases, the new artefact, called a User Interface Specification, was introduced. This proved to be a double-edged sword. On one side, it allowed the product analysts to concentrate on workflow and non-functional requirements without getting hung up in solutions. On the other side, it took away parts of their traditional tasks and responsibilities. We had to put a lot of emphasis on collaboration and shared ownership of a complete analysis package to convey the message that the product analysts would still have a big say in the definition of the user interface, and the initial work was more educational and focused on obtaining buy-in rather than looking merely at the analysis work. Eventually this was perceived as a valid and helpful distinction of specification documents, with experience being the biggest comfort factor.

During the roll-out of the new process the product analysts realised that they weren't used to performing requirement analysis in such a holistic way and would benefit from additional training, so we brought in experts to educate them in contextual inquiry as an analysis method. Having a common framework like contextual inquiry helped a lot in all following projects, as it made clear to everybody what the purpose and usage of their analysis work is going to be.

The collaboration between product analyst and UI designer has been carried all the way through the Elaboration phase and often ended up being an almost symbiotic relationship with very close cooperation. In order to extend the knowledge to the downstream organisation (the development team), the work mode of collaboration was also introduced at the handover point between the elaboration and build phases. In these sessions, the developers and testers on the development side were walked through the complete body of analysis for a given project or module in order to ensure unambiguous and complete understanding on the development side.

The second level of process roll-out was to establish ownership and decision authority. In a large enterprise such as ours, this is a crucial element of process introduction. Many 'best practice' processes such as the International Standards Organisation's ISO-9000/9001 standards (www.iso.org/iso/en/iso9000-14000/index.html) and the Software Engineering Institute's Capability Maturity Model Integration (CMMI; see www.sei.cmu.edu/cmmi/) call for requirements and their effect on subsequent designs to be traceable throughout documents or repositories. Accordingly, in our organisation, the various stakeholders write up their results and relate them to existing requirements. Usually, a review and release process is applied to prevent errors from occurring in the process or from being identified too late. Considering these factors, we proceeded in two directions.

First, we introduced the UI Specification (owned by the UI design team) as a new mandatory artefact in the company's Quality Management System (QMS). We convinced the QMS group of its benefit for ensuring traceability of workflow and UI requirements through the process and, after getting their buy-in, received outstanding support for ensuring compliance in the organisation.

As a second route, we established review and approval authority. As our documents were reviewed and approved by a multitude of stakeholders, we asked to be included as reviewers for those documents that govern our work (both project- and product-related). Everybody could see the benefit of that and gladly received our feedback.

After merely giving feedback for a few months, we asked to be made document approvers (in contrast to just reviewers, i.e. without our approval the document cannot be released). The request was granted for the key documents we make use of for our portion of the work (e.g. Use Cases, Project Plan etc.). By these means, we have moved the UI team's role from one of mainly support through providing helpful feedback towards being approvers and thus co-decision makers of the direction a product and the respective project takes, which ensures a UI focus on almost all levels of product and project planning.

While implementing the new user-centred design process we encountered quite a few obstacles. But we also encountered enablers and supporters. We summarise the obstacles and the enablers below.

Tradition, pride, and the presence of any existing process, product or model usually ranked very high in the list of obstacles. We still encounter situations where we are confronted with a statement such as 'Our system ABC provides this feature in that way and the users want it exactly that way', although much less frequently today than initially, when each and every design was challenged and compared to the legacy systems. The same was true for methods and documentation, where we were frequently directed to legacy documents (e.g. feature lists without any workflow) and expected to work from those, instead of conducting a comprehensive user and task analysis. The same was true for legacy systems ('just make it work like XYZ').

On the other side, we had a lot of support from various areas in the organisation while implementing the new process. The two strongest supporters were upper management and quality management. Upper management had to be convinced that the change would actually improve product quality and requested regular updates on progress. They needed to see the advantages before they acted to change the organisational framework (in terms of headcount, reporting structure, roles) and to communicate the changes to the affected teams.

Quality management's main goal as a group is to establish repeatable and manageable processes throughout the organisation. Consequently, they were very open to supporting our approach – especially as it was more structured than a generic feature-based analysis process – and willingly included us and the UI perspective in every planning or change-of-process discussion.

By utilising these two groups, we were able to drive the process forward. It is still not perfect, but it is a great leap forward for an organisation that bought into innovation and user focus on a very fundamental level.

AND WHERE WE WANT TO GO

There will always be additional tasks that can be added and process elements that can be optimised. For a living and ongoing project, this is always the norm rather than the exception. We currently have a few of topics on our radar:

- We want to broaden the applicability area for our process to the complete organisation, making sure that all new products in the medical software domain are developed with the strong user focus we applied to our projects. As we can show more and more success stories with every new product or release and positive customer feedback, this is becoming easier every time. We currently have one project per month contacting us and asking for process and product support in one way or another.

- For our core projects, we want to establish UI analysis more formally in our requirement engineering process, especially with regard to tool support. Currently, the feature analysis documents are decomposed into single traceable requirements in a single repository that is used for scoping, generating automated test cases and tracking development progress. We want the same level of decomposition for the UI-specific requirements and therefore will move towards decomposing our artefacts in the same way.

- Last but not least there is a growing need for support and tools for the downstream organisations within the development teams that usually don't consist of skilled UI designers. Repositories and reference sites are currently being implemented to provide a central location to access all UI-related information. This will relieve every single UI designer on the team who currently has to address requests for e.g. icons, graphics and style guides from a variety of stakeholders in development, testing and neighbouring areas.

Taking all of this together we feel that we have achieved a solid base for user-centred design in our organisation. While continuing to evolve and optimise our approach, the fundamental perception throughout the organisation has changed towards seeing UI design as an integral part of every analysis effort and the UI team as a key player in a sustainable and profitable product development process.

REFERENCE

Hacker, W. (1994). *Action Regulation Theory and occupational psychology: review of German empirical research since 1987*. The German Journal of Psychology 18(2), 91–120.

CHAPTER 9

Collaborating with Change Agents to Make a Better User Interface

Paul Sherman and Susan L. Hura

When was the last time you called a customer service or technical support line and tried to escape from the company's automated phone system? Notice we didn't say 'Have you ever …?' We assume everyone eventually tries to skip the 'interactive voice response' system, or IVRs as they're known, and attempts to get to a live person.

Why is this so common?

Because many IVRs are not usable. Their prompts are not always understandable to ordinary people because they use unfamiliar terminology. Sometimes the prompts are just too darned long, and by the end of the prompt you've forgotten what the voice said at the beginning. Other times the menu structure is so impenetrably deep or convoluted, you become lost.

So why are many IVR user interfaces so poorly designed?

We're sure you've guessed the answer: they weren't designed by people who know about people's limited ability to retain information received via the auditory channel (that is, through the ears). The people who design the prompts and menu structures are often the same people who staff and manage the call centre. They know what issues people call about, but they can't really be expected to know about people's cognitive limitations, or be familiar with user-centred design techniques such as prototyping, usability testing and iterative design.

In this chapter, we'll describe our analysis of an IVR for the technical support line of a professional accounting software application, our redesign of the IVR and the outcome of the redesign. We'll also relate how we got the opportunity to carry out this project, and what organisational factors influenced the project.

First, some background.

THE SITUATION

For some software organisations, providing technical support for their complex or premium-priced applications represents a significant portion of the cost of doing business. Understandably, these organisations are motivated to minimise these costs whenever possible.

In 2002, one of us (Sherman) was working at a company that produced a high-priced tax-return-preparation application marketed to professional tax preparers such as Certified Public Accountants. It came to light during conversations with representatives of the support organisation that approximately 13 per cent of callers to the technical support line were choosing the wrong path through the IVR system, and routing themselves to the wrong support team.

This created a non-optimal customer experience for the customers. During the height of the tax season, customers called often. The support staff had a very good reputation; the customers felt that the support reps really 'knew their stuff' and could help them deal with particularly complex tax returns as well as issues related to the application itself. Also, the company did not charge customers for technical support. For the customers, the tech support line was an all-you-can-eat smorgasbord of advice and assistance. The downside was that, like the buffet line at a crowded reception, customers often waited in a queue for many minutes before getting to a rep with a good knowledge of the particular issue they were calling about.

For those 13 per cent of callers who went to the wrong queue, the wait was often doubled. They would make a choice from the IVR menu, and be funnelled into a queue leading to a particular group of reps. Because no rep could possibly be conversant in every area of the application and each particular topic related to tax preparation, management had grouped the support reps into skill teams. One team fielded all the hardware, software and networking-related calls. One handled only questions about business tax. Another covered individual tax. Still another dealt with state tax issues.

As a result, the unlucky 13 per cent would be greeted by a rep, and would begin to describe their problems. As soon as they made their issue clear to the rep, they would be told that they would have to be transferred to a different support team. And then they would be put back in the queue.

This wasn't just annoying to the customer. It also lengthened the per-call handle time for the support organisation, reducing its efficiency and adding to its costs. When management assessed the impact of these wrong-queue/transfer calls, it turned out they were costing the company about USUS$185 000 yearly.

LET'S DO SOMETHING ABOUT IT

Sherman got to talking with Thad, a Six Sigma Black Belt working on ways to reduce costs in the support department. Wikipedia (http://en.wikipedia. org) defines 'Six Sigma' as a conceptual outlook and set of processes originally formulated to achieve quality in manufacturing operations. Popularised at Motorola and GE in the late 1980s and early 1990s, it spread to software and services companies in the mid-1990s.

Six Sigma's core concepts involve estimating the defect rate of a process by sampling the output of the process, counting the defective output, and calculating the defect rate, assuming a normal distribution of defects. The derived number (for example, 2 defective parts per million parts manufactured) corresponds to a certain number of standard deviations (or 'sigmas') away from the mean. (The mean represents the defects which would be found if there were no attempts to control quality.) The term 'Six Sigma' refers to a defect rate of 1 in 3.4 million or less, which corresponds to six standard deviations from the mean.

Six Sigma practitioners undergo training in statistical methods and quality control, offered by a number of vendors around the world. Beginning practitioners are termed 'Green Belts'; more experienced practitioners earn the (hard to say with a straight face) title 'Black Belt' and 'Master Black Belt'.

Thad, who was responsible for improving processes and realising cost savings in the support centre, described the wrong-queue/transfer issue, wondering if there were ways to address it. As a user-centred design (UCD) practitioner, it sounded to me as if callers were misunderstanding the menu options, and routing themselves to the wrong group of reps by mistake. Thad said it was plausible, but offered competing hypotheses:

- Callers were trying to 'game' the system, making menu selections they thought would take them to a shorter queue.

- Thirteen per cent was the 'structural' error rate; nothing could be done to lower it.

We offered to take a look at (or, more accurately, a listen to) the system to assess whether the wrong-queue/transfer rate may be due to a poor user interface. Thad asked how much time and effort it would take on our part. After a quick consultation with the other members of the UCD team, we estimated that we could perform a usability review of the system, identify issues that may be causing callers to select the wrong menu option, and write up our results and recommendations in about 25–30 hours.

Applying usability engineering methods to this problem was a risk. Although this company had a strong user-centred design culture for its desktop and web-based software products, it had no previous experience of applying UCD to other areas of the customer experience such as the support centre.

In addition, as in most organisations, this company's different functional groups were somewhat insular. We discovered that Thad was meeting some resistance from support management simply because they were not familiar with Six Sigma methods. Although Six Sigma and process improvement was being advocated for from the highest levels of the company, practitioners sometimes encountered resistance because they were not as familiar with the particular domain as were the staff and management. This resistance sometimes manifested itself in the implicit attitude of 'We don't need you; we can solve our own problems.'

Introducing yet another 'expert' into the mix, one whose main competencies were software user interfaces, was a gamble. But in the end, Thad decided to green-light our (UCD's) analysis. Why? We like to think it was because our focus on gathering data, analysing it, and generating data-driven recommendations was in line with the Six Sigma approach. More likely, Thad probably gambled that letting us do an analysis wouldn't hurt; if we came up with good information, he'd continue utilising us. If we didn't come up with anything compelling and actionable, he could easily tell us 'Thanks for your input; we'll call you if we need anything more.'

So we performed an analysis of the IVR system's user interface, wrote it up and, together with Thad, presented our results to the support centre's senior management.

Before we tell you about that meeting, we will tell you what we found in our analysis.

THE ANALYSIS

We took two distinct approaches during the analysis. First, the prompts and menu structure were subjected to a heuristic evaluation, a relatively inexpensive usability evaluation method whereby a practitioner or several practitioners examine a user interface and determine its conformance to established usability principles (Nielsen and Molich, 1990; Nielsen 1994).

The IVR prompts and menu structure (also referred to as 'call flows') were evaluated using two sets of heuristics. One set, developed by Nielsen and Molich (1990) and Nielsen (1994), has been widely used in evaluations of desktop and web-based software user interfaces. The heuristics used from this set are summarised below:

- visibility of system status – the system should keep user apprised of its status;

- match between system and real world - use words, concepts and phrases that are familiar to the user;

- user control and freedom – provide users with the ability to undo actions and recover from undesired states;

- consistency and standards – use terms and actions consistently;

- error prevention – design the system so that users are prevented from committing errors;

- recognition rather than recall – design so that users do not have to remember information from one area of the system to another;

- flexibility and efficiency of use – provide accelerators and short cuts to aid the more experienced user;

- error recognition, diagnosis, and recovery – help users recognise, diagnose, and recover from errors.

A second set of heuristics specific to voice-user interfaces was developed by Hura (2003), based upon the results of usability tests with IVRs and speech recognition applications. They overlap somewhat with Nielsen's (1994) heuristics, but they provide distinct utility for evaluations of voice-user interfaces, particularly speech-recognition applications. The heuristics relevant to this evaluation are paraphrased below:

- Match the caller's expectations and understanding of the domain – ensure that the system reflects the caller's understanding of and terminology used in the domain.

- Minimise the limitations of the medium – since auditory memory is severely limited and quite transient, system navigation and the design of prompts should be simple and easily retained.

- Help the caller avoid errors and recover from errors gracefully – provide ways for callers to obtain advice when they are likely to need it, and allow callers to change their minds or make corrections to input.

- Make the caller comfortable using the technology – ensure that the caller is comfortable enough to use the system instead of attempting to bypass it and speak to a live representative.

In the second part of the analysis, we examined the prompts, with attention to the source and destination of these wrong-queue/transfer calls. That is, rather than simply evaluating the prompts and menus 'in a vacuum', we attempted to establish to what support queues callers initially (and incorrectly) routed themselves, and to what queues they were transferred.

Doing this helped us identify the most common failure paths callers followed through the IVR. We then examined the wording of the prompts callers heard when they made the wrong choice.

THE RESULTS

Our analysis revealed five main issues. Table 9.1 summarises the issues as well as the heuristic related to each issue.

NO 'KEY-OVER'

The IVR system did not provide callers with the ability to navigate back to a previous menu. As callers listened to prompts and made choices, they were stuck with their choices, and had no ability to recover from a mistake and navigate back up to the next highest level of the menu hierarchy. This capability is usually referred to as 'key-over'.

Not providing key-over when in a queue essentially forces the caller to hang up and redial if they mistakenly end up in the wrong queue. Providing this ability to callers affords people more control over the application, and can help callers recover from mistakes and slips (e.g., attempting to choose option '4' but instead pushing '1' or '7' on the keypad).

NO SUPPORT FOR PRE-EMPTIVE CALLER INPUT ('BARGE-IN')

The system did not allow callers to 'barge-in' while a prompt was playing in order to skip the remainder of a prompt. The system also did not provide barge-in during the welcome message. Barge-in is desirable when callers

Table 9.1   Issues identified and heuristic violated
(adapted from Sherman, 2003)

Issue	Heuristics Violated
Inadequate key-over - no opportunity for callers to navigate back to a previous menu level (e.g., 'To go back to the previous menu, press 9').	User control and freedom; Error recognition, diagnosis and recovery; Help the caller avoid and recover from errors.
No support for pre-emptive caller input during prompts (i.e., 'barge-in').	User control and freedom; Flexibility and efficiency of use.
No repeat - callers were not able to repeat prompts (e.g., 'To hear this menu again, press star').	User control and freedom; Error recognition, diagnosis and recovery; Help the caller avoid and recover from errors.
Some prompts were too long, or combined multiple options into a single, difficult-to-understand prompt.	Recognition rather than recall; Minimize the limitations of the medium.
Several adjacent prompts contained too-similar terms.	Minimize the limitations of the medium.

are familiar with a system and don't want to wait for a prompt to complete. Recall that most customers called several times each year; some customers called dozens of times during the tax season. Forcing these callers to listen to 'Welcome!' verbiage and prompts they have already heard was very likely to frustrate them.

NO REPEAT

Callers were not able to repeat prompts (e.g., 'To hear this menu again, press star'). Information entering into short-term or 'working' memory via the auditory channel tends to decay (that is, to be forgotten) fairly quickly (Cowan, 1984). Repeating a prompt gives callers the ability to compensate for the limitations of auditory memory. They can double-check the content of a prompt if they are unsure whether it's the correct choice, or if they have forgotten the contents of the prompt.

OVERLY LONG AND COMBINED PROMPTS

Some prompts were quite long or combined multiple options into a single prompt. An example of a long prompt included the following:

- 'For system-related questions, including modem communications, program installation, networks, printers and error messages, press 3.'

This and other long prompts were likely to 'overload' callers' auditory memory capacity. This overload, combined with callers' inability to repeat prompts, could lead them to make incorrect choices.

Several prompts combined multiple concepts into a single difficult-to-understand message. These prompts were probably confusing to callers. When listening to compound prompts, some people may only attend to the first part of the message, and fail to remember the second part (this is known as the primacy effect). Others will forget the first part, and only recall the last part of the prompt (this is known as the recency effect) (Baddeley and Hitch, 1993).

Examples of compound prompts included these:

- 'For questions regarding your licence renewal, changes to your existing account, or other non-technical questions, press 1.'

- 'For the status of previously filed electronic returns and for program installation questions, press 5.'

- 'For questions regarding modem communications or electronic filing acknowledgement information, press 1.'

There was no good reason for these items to be grouped together. When we asked the support staff why they grouped, say, modem communications together with electronic filing acknowledgement, we got the answer we suspected – these issues were handled by the same skill area.

ADJACENT PROMPTS WITH TOO-SIMILAR TERMS

At several places within the system, two adjacent messages contained similar terms. We felt that callers may have trouble discriminating between the two when listening to them sequentially. Examples of similar adjacent prompts include the following:

- 'For the status of previously filed electronic returns and for program installation questions, press 5.'

- 'For product technical support and all other electronic filing questions, press 6.'

These adjacent prompts both mention electronic filing. This could lead to confusion for callers who have a question about electronic filing, but are unsure whether 'option 6' covers all electronic filing questions, or just questions about returns that have not yet been electronically filed.

Another example of adjacent prompts with similar content is below:

- 'For tax-related and program operation questions, press 1.'

- 'For 1040 electronic filing questions, press 2.'

The first prompt makes mention of 'tax-related' questions, but the second prompt mentions '1040', which is certainly a tax-related term.

THE PITCH

Armed with a short write-up and a PowerPoint presentation, we met with support centre management to discuss our analysis.

Thad started the meeting by reviewing the problem we were attempting to solve, his mission to find cost savings and efficiencies in the support centre, and his decision to utilise a team of usability engineers from the product development area of the company to assess the IVR user interface.

We then presented our findings, taking care to point out several positive aspects of the system. We mentioned that voice talent's tone was pleasing; the system's voice showed good enunciation and was not overly formal. We also pointed out that the menu structure struck a good balance between depth and breadth; it was neither too deep nor too shallow, and there were rarely more than four options at any level. Finally, we mentioned that this provided callers with an efficient means of getting to certain options. Depending on their goal, callers could get into a queue in as few as two key presses.

We reviewed our method, and provided some background on auditory memory and aural-user interfaces. Then we gave them the 'Your baby is ugly' news. We told them in detail what was wrong with their system, and why. To their credit, they listened to the information with equanimity, asking only clarifying questions.

We then described our recommendations for redesigning the IVR user interface. We proposed providing additional capabilities, revising or eliminating certain prompts, adding some new prompts, and slightly modifying the menu structure. Our recommendations could be boiled down to these points:

- add barge-in, key-over, and repeat

- shorten most prompts

- use terms that will be familiar to the caller

- disentangle and split compound (multiple option) prompts.

We then launched into a discussion about whether they wanted to proceed with the redesign, and how we could test the redesigned system before putting it into service.

We offered the customer support team several options. The first option was to redesign the IVR user interface, and put it into service in parallel with the existing IVR. Callers would be randomly assigned to either the existing or redesigned IVR. After a small but statistically large-enough sample was gathered, we would remove the redesigned IVR from service while the wrong-queue/transfer rates for each design were analysed.

The second option we offered was to test the redesign in tandem with the existing design. In tandem testing, we would specify a time period during which the redesign was in service, and another time period during which the existing design was in service. Each IVR would remain in service for the same number of days and during the same days of the week, to eliminate any bias that may occur as a result of peak support days, difference in support staffing or other factors. To correct for unequal sample sizes across the comparison periods, we would compare the ratio of number of calls transferred with the number of calls taken in each sample. This would allow comparison of unequal sample sizes.

The third option we offered was to simply put the redesign into service, and measure the wrong-queue/transfer rate going forward against the historical wrong-queue/transfer rate. We did not favour this option because it did not allow us to test before committing to the redesigned system.

To our initial surprise, they chose the third option. The support team explained that their IVR system did not allow them to test in parallel, as they had no ability to put two different user interfaces into service simultaneously. They also did not want to test in tandem because they believed their IVR system did not posses a staging area where they could save the existing prompts, and put them back in service at a later time. They believed that they would have had to re-record the voice prompts, which costs money.

So they chose the cheapest yet riskiest option. We began our redesign the next day.

THE REDESIGN

We began the redesign by documenting the global changes we recommended – barge-in, key-over, and repeat prompt capabilities. We shortened most messages. We replaced several terms in use in the application that we thought were causing confusion. We disentangled and split compound prompts. For example, consider these two prompts:

- 'For the status of previously filed electronic returns and for program installation questions, press 5.'

- 'For product technical support and all other electronic filing questions, press 6.'

We split up the two above prompts into these four:

- 'To check the status of previously filed electronic returns, press 1.'

- 'For all other electronic filing questions, press 2.'

- 'For assistance with installing the program, press 3.'

- 'For all other technical support questions, press 4.'

We met with the stakeholders from the support team to review the redesign. After some minor tweaks, we scheduled a cut over date, and the support team sent the new design off to be recorded by a voice talent. The redesigned system went live on 3 June 2002.

THE OUTCOMES

So what happened? Happily, the wrong-queue/transfer rate fell from 13.5 per cent to 8 per cent in the first few days, and finally settled at 4.5 per cent after several weeks. We had succeeded in lowering the wrong-queue/transfer rate by nearly two-thirds.

After we were confident that the rate had stayed low, we calculated the return on investment for the project. Using methods that are documented by Bias and Mayhew in their seminal work 'Cost-Justifying Usability' (1994), we estimated that the costs associated with the time devoted to the project by two usability professionals worked out to about US$2500. This was based on a fully-loaded headcount rate of US$160000 per year / 1,920 hours = US$83.33 dollars per hour, multiplied by approximately 30 hours. The cost of the stakeholders' time and voice talent was pegged at somewhere between US$3300 and US$3750. Using the higher estimate yielded a total cost of US$6250.

Thad and the support team projected the yearly cost savings associated with the reduced wrong-queue/transfer rate, and came up with a figure of US$58000 per year. This led us to estimate a first-year benefit-to-cost ratio of 9.25 to 1. Benefits would of course continue to accrue year over year, provided the wrong-queue/transfer rate remained low.

LESSONS, HELPS AND HINDRANCES

This project was a noteworthy story about how usability engineering and user-centred design techniques were employed to solve a problem in an area that was not typically serviced by user-centred design practitioners. It's also a story about how practitioners from two disparate yet related disciplines came together to craft a collaborative approach to a problem and solve it through a combination of technical skills and 'soft' skills.

If any lessons can be extracted from our experience, one is that large businesses can derive substantial benefits when people from different disciplines have the opportunity to meet, learn about and collaborate with each other. Such cross-discipline knowledge sharing and collaboration is often a precursor for the development and implementation of new approaches to long-standing or irritating problems.

Another lesson this project may impart is that when you're acting as a change agent, it is very easy to step on others' toes. While it's gratifying to drive change in your organisation, it's even more rewarding to drive change without leaving a trail of bruised feelings in your wake. There were times when we – both UCD and Six Sigma practitioners – came on too strong with the support team. It was partly due to our excitement at being on the trail of an interesting problem. But, and this is difficult to admit, it was probably driven by some amount of arrogance as well – after all, we were the experts, we had the answers, we knew what was wrong and how to fix their mistakes. And this put off the support team at times. We managed to rein in our more arrogant behaviour before we caused irreparable damage to the relationship, but our attitudes and behaviours were no doubt barriers to the support team's initial acceptance of our approach, findings and recommendations.

Our other learning points were standard fare: when reaching out to another group, it's important to learn their terminology, and how they measure their successes. Then couch the business case for your project in terms that have meaning and value to the stakeholders.

Finally, this initiative was yet another reminder that it's important to practise good project management. We made sure to write a project charter, and described the deliverables and success criteria for the project. We also created a schedule and communicated it to the stakeholders. Finally, we explicitly defined both our and the stakeholders' responsibilities, and ensured that the responsibilities were acknowledged by the members of the support team.

This was a small, bounded project. But we believe that the real value of this project shouldn't be measured by size. It should be measured by the success we experienced in forging cross-discipline relationships, and in discovering how UCD and other disciplines like Six Sigma can complement and leverage the others' strengths and capabilities.

REFERENCES

Baddeley, A.D., and Hitch, G. (1993). *The Recency Effect: Implicit Learning with Explicit Retrieval?* Memory and Cognition, 21, 146–55.

Bias, R.G., and Mayhew, D.J. (1994). *Cost-Justifying Usability*. San Diego, CA: Academic Press.

Cowan, N. (1984). *On Short and Long Auditory Stores*. Psychological Bulletin, 96, 341–370.

Hura, S.L. (2003). *Heuristics: Lessons in the Art of Automated Conversation*. Retrieved March 4, 2003 from http://216.162.203.249/downloads/Intervoice_Heuristics_Article_1.7.03.doc.

Nielsen, J. (1994). *Heuristic Evaluation*. In Nielsen, J., and Mack, R.L. (Eds.), Usability Inspection Methods. John Wiley & Sons, New York, NY.

Nielsen, J., and Molich, R. (1990). *Heuristic Evaluation of User Interfaces*. Proceedings of the ACM CHI 1990 Conference. (Seattle, WA, 1–5 April), 249–256.

Sherman, P.J. (2003). *Redesign of a Technical Support Interactive Voice Response*

System: Applying Heuristics to Business Problems. Proceedings of the Human Factors and Ergonomics Society 47th Annual Meeting, 774–777.

Wikipedia (2005). *Six Sigma*. Retrieved from http://en.wikipedia.org/wiki/Six_Sigma, December, 2005.

CHAPTER 10

Learning from Success Stories

Paul Sherman

The stories you've read in this book have been about how focusing on usability makes a difference in how software applications and websites are created. They've also been about the struggles and successes that usability and user-centred design practitioners encounter as they work with business people and technologists in fast-paced, high-stakes projects.

So what can we learn from this collection of experiences?

As I reviewed the authors' stories, I began to see a common theme: successful application of user-centred design and usability initially takes hold in the margins. UCD practitioners often start to change their organisations in those fuzzy areas between the disciplines, the region where informal discussions and agreements arise between people working together, yet are not written up and formalised in a process document or workflow description.

In these margins, dedicated practitioners with both technical skills and the patience and tenacity to influence others strive to identify and understand where users find it difficult to accomplish their goals. These agents of change describe the problems, their implications, the probable cost to the organisation of fixing versus not fixing them, then advocate ways to alleviate or solve the problems.

When they gain sufficient influence to effect change – both to designs and the processes used to create and implement designs – their efforts are rewarded. When systems are redesigned – or even better – designed from the ground up to align with users' mental models, users can find what they need on the website, route themselves to the right technical support rep, successfully create an invoice or perform an analysis of financial data.

Typically, leaders within organisations notice when the application of user-centred design methods leads to a clear success, such as a dramatic rise in customer sales or a decrease in incorrectly-routed calls. At this point, people with little prior exposure to UCD become 'UCD evangelists' and, along with UCD practitioners, seek to drive UCD into the design and development process.

But changing an organisation's established processes is usually a long, hard slog, especially in large organisations. Processes exist in large organisations to help reduce ambiguity and ensure that operations can continue despite the loss of any one individual playing a role in a design and development process. To a certain extent the processes that organisations put in place – the way they organise work and specify how groups of people communicate and coordinate – is a large component of the organisation's culture. Researchers who specialise in studying organisational cultures, such as Geert Hofstede (1991) and Jim Collins (2001), point out that when organisational cultures change at all, they change slowly.

But organisational cultures can and do change, sometimes significantly. With enough advocacy and influence, key people in high-level management positions, technical thought leaders who aren't high ranking but nonetheless are seen as 'go-to' people, and dedicated individuals on the business side can move an organisation from its current state to a desired future state. It is in these situations that organisational cultures change to accommodate user-centred design concepts, methods and techniques. The activities that usability practitioners previously carried out 'in the margins' take a more-central role. And the organisation becomes more focused on the users of the technology, and less focused on itself.

In the most user-focused organisations, user-centred design activities and usability testing become 'non-optional' steps in the process. The organisation evolves its design and development processes to include explicit, required steps where data from users are gathered and used to improve designs and identify new or misunderstood user needs. Speaking from experience, it's a joy to watch an organisation transform in this manner.

Not all of the organisations described in these stories have achieved this high level of UCD integration. Most, in fact, are still working out exactly how user-centred design fits within their processes and organisational culture. And they're also figuring out what types of people make the most effective change agents. From our years of experience working as change agents and watching our colleagues serve in similar roles, the other authors and I have found that effective change agents in our discipline are similar in that they:

- reach across discipline boundaries, identify like-minded change agents and build relationships to foster collaboration;

- are persistent in their advocacy of a data-driven approach to design;

- possess the ability to patiently yet inexorably work around resistance and organisational obstacles;

- demonstrate in both words and actions a passionate belief that technology should serve users and not the other way around;

- have a strong grounding in business and technology;

- have empathy for others who do not (yet) share their vision and passion about user-centred design, but don't evince a superior or patronising attitude toward colleagues who don't share their views.

This last characteristic is critical. By definition, user-centred design establishes a relationship of 'creative tension' between the business representatives who typically want the product to contain every conceivable feature, the technologists who often have strongly held ideas about how to build the product's user interfaces, and the UCD practitioner who seeks to discover what the target user group really needs (and represent these needs in the design).

The UCD practitioner's role as user advocate can sometimes cause them to discount the value of the business representative and the technologists' contributions. In these situations, the UCD practitioner can come across as smug, superior and too critical. When the other disciplines perceive UCD practitioners in this way, their effectiveness is vastly reduced.

Nothing illustrates this unfortunate situation better than the words of my father, an electrical engineer and computer scientist. One day in the late 1980s, while he was driving me back to college from a visit home, I told him I was interested in moving from clinical psychology to applied psychology. I told him that I had run across some papers from a group of psychologists at Bell Laboratories, where he had worked for almost my entire life on a number of telecommunications software and hardware products.

'Yeah, you probably don't want to hear what those psychologists have to say,' he said with more than a bit of a sneer. 'Why?' I asked. His answer: 'They all act like their **** doesn't stink.'

My father did not often curse. For him to let loose like that meant that he held this particular group of colleagues in especially low regard. It wasn't until years later that I understood that this was a clear sign that those applied psychologists at Bell Labs, no matter how academically accomplished they were, were probably not effective collaborators or change agents within Bell Labs.

So what can a product or services organisation learn from the stories we've told here? For organisations looking to become more user-centred, the message is simple: strive to hire practitioners who play well with others, yet have the tenacity to stand up for the data. Try to get people who are comfortable in the role of incrementally inching an organisation forward. Don't accept practitioners who claim to have the answer; instead, look for practitioners who are comfortable saying, 'I don't know, but I can find out the answer, or at least give you several options, and it'll take me two weeks and ten users.'

Let's say that an organisation has hired UCD practitioners with desirable characteristics. At this point, success is far from certain. Even the best practitioners will have limited or no effect if the organisation doesn't change and adapt to the methods, processes and data that the UCD practitioner brings to the table. What can decision makers do to increase the likelihood that user-centred design will take root in their organisation?

The lessons from these stories should be clear. The authors' stories, my own included, indicate that user-centred design needs to be integrated firmly and thoughtfully into the design and development process. You can't just wave a magic usability wand at a product before it ships and have it come out usable. Adapting user-centred design to your processes is a disruptive exercise, with many unknowns. If there are lessons to be learned from these stories, one important one is that decision makers and UCD champions need to be comfortable with ambiguity. Champions are indispensable for the trails they blaze and the obstacles they remove. But when the people doing the work actually convene to figure out how to 'do' UCD in their particular environment, the champion needs to let the cross-discipline teams work out exactly how UCD should be done in their particular environment.

In some organisations, it makes sense to do what some of the contributors describe, namely to fully specify who does what, and when. In other organisations, a less-prescriptive, looser process may work best.

The key is to be flexible when creating a more user-focused organisation. Evaluate different approaches. Let the individuals who will be doing the 'real' work figure out how to strike a balance between incorporating user data and moving rapidly enough to get products out the door and into the market. Set expectations in your organisation that, while it may take some time to work out the best way to incorporate user data into design and validation, the increased focus on users is not just another 'management fad' but a core value of the organisation.

In my professional life (and, I admit, in my personal beliefs as well), I am ecumenical. There are many right ways to do things, many paths to the truth. There are also many ways that business stakeholders, technologists, UCD practitioners and champions of UCD can foster a user-centred organisation. If anyone comes along claiming that they have 'the' solution that applies equally well to all organisations, you should run away!

In closing, I want to share my hope that these success stories will provide you with some initial directions as you seek to make your organisation more focused on the customer. I firmly believe that the experience and knowledge of a dozen practitioners is much more useful than the pronouncements of any single UCD guru. I hope I am proved right, and you benefit from the many perspectives and opinions contained in this book.

REFERENCES

Collins, J. (2001). *Good to Great: Why Some Companies Make the Leap... and Others Don't*. New York: HarperCollins.

Hofstede, G. (1991). *Cultures and Organizations: Software Of The Mind*. Maidenhead, U.K: McGraw-Hill.

Index

advertising
importance in web redesign, 82-3,
83
analysis, data
process in web redesign, 75-6
analysis, 'feature function/value'
role within project management,
141-4
analysis, user interface
experience at Siemens, 169-75
Anita (case study)
working relationship conflict resolution, 96-110, *106*
appeal, visual
importance in web redesign, 82-3,
83
architects, information (IAs)
case study of role, 139-50, *141, 145,
148*
definition and characteristics, 135-7
value to project management, 150-
51
arizonajeans.com, 41-2
assessment, situation
importance of reflection, 95-6, *95*

Bell Laboratories, 193-4
BigVine, 29, *34*
brainstorming
strategy for successful relationships,
96
branding
importance in web redesign, 82-3,
83
Brian (case study)
working relationship conflict
resolution, 96-110, *106*
budgets, project

need for planning, 138-9
bureaucracies, organisation of
barrier to E-government delivery,
72-3
threat to web redesign, 87
'busy-ness', appearance of
barrier to project completion, 137

calculations
facilitation following ease of use
metrics, 30-31, *32*
CARD approach
to IMS design, 122-3
case studies *see name or subject eg* Chris;
interactive voice response
systems; Remedy Software
change, organisational
importance of personal credibility,
54-6
prioritisation, 56-7
role of project validation, 58
characteristics, personal
obstacles/enablers to design
implementation, 173-4
Chris (case study)
working relationship conflict
resolution, 96-110, *106*
citizenry, diversity of
barrier to E-government delivery,
73-4
clarification, problem
strategy for successful relationships,
96
clients, business intelligence
role in project development,
113-14
use in IMS design, 130-31
collaboration, group

importance in conflict resolution,
    109-10
colleagues, workplace
    importance in relationship
        cultivation, 59, 93-4
collection, data
    process in web redesign, 75-6
Collins, J., 192
commitment, collective
    strategy for successful relationships,
        96
communication, project findings
    process at SAS, 117-21, *118, 120*
communication, inter-personal
    importance in conflict resolution,
        107
competition, inter-departmental
    threat to web redesign, 88
'concept phase', user interface design,
    160-62, *161*
conflicts, workplace
    case study, 96-110, *106*
    strategies for resolution, 105-110,
        106
    threat to web redesign success, 64
consultants (advice consultants)
    importance of relationship
        cultivation, 59-60
content, web site
    find and verifying, 84-7
contradiction, factual
    threat to web redesign, 88
cooperation, decision-making
    importance in conflict resolution,
        109
counsel and support, external
    importance in conflict resolution,
        108-9
credibility, personal
    importance when effecting change,
        54-6
cube data/OLAP manipulation, 122
cultures, organisational
    characteristics and challenges, 16-20

impact on efficiency and outputs,
    9-10
see also types eg. 'customer oriented';
    'design oriented'; 'engineer
    oriented'
'customer oriented' cultures
    characteristics, 19-20
    response to ease of use metrics
        adoption, 35-6, *36*
customers, business intelligence
    role in project development,
        113-14
    use in IMS design, 130-31

data, collection and analysis
    process in web redesign, 75-6
Debbie (case study)
    working relationship conflict
        resolution, 96-110, *106*
design, asynchronous collaborative
    advantages and disadvantages, *125,
        133*
    experience with IMS project, 123-31,
        124, 125, 127, 129
design, user-centred
    advantages of adoption, 191-5
    characteristics and importance, 4-5
    IMS case study, 111-31, *118, 121,
        124, 125, 127, 129*
    role, 7-8
design, user interface
    experience at Siemens, 169-75
    organisational challenges, 168-9
    process of, 159-68, *161, 163, 164,
        165*
    see also designers, user-centred;
        teams, user interface design
design and redesign, web site *see*
        web sites, redesign
'design oriented' cultures
    characteristics, 18-19
    response to 'ease of use metrics'
        adoption, 33-5, *34*
designers, interaction

importance of understanding
    colleagues, 93-4
personal qualities required, 59-61,
    192-3
role, 1-2, 7-8
designers, user-centred
    importance of understanding col-
        leagues, 93-4
    personal qualities required, 59-61,
        173-4, 192-3
    role, 1-2, 155-6, *156*
    see also teams, user interface design
dissemination, project findings
    process at SAS, 117-21, *118, 120*
distrust
    barrier to project completion, 137
drafting
    user interface design process, 164-6,
        165
duplication, information
    threat to web redesign, 88

E-government
    barriers to successful delivery, 72-4
    definition (USA), 65
    drivers for extension of, 67-72, *68,*
        69
E-government Act, 2002 (USA), 70-71
'ease of use' metrics
    adoption by organisations, 32-6, *33,*
        34, 36
    benefits, 23-31, *32*
    characteristics, 21-3, *22, 23*
effectiveness
    role of ease of use metrics, 21-3, *22,*
        23
efficiency
    impact of organisational cultures,
        9-10
    role of ease of use metrics, 21-3, *22,*
        23
'elaboration phase', user interface de-
        sign, 162-8, *163, 164, 165*
electronic government

barriers to successful delivery, 72-4
definition (USA), 65
drivers for extension of, 67-72, *68,*
    69
Ellen (case study)
    working relationship conflict
        resolution, 96-110, *106*
employees, business intelligence
    lack as hindrance to project
        development, 113-14
end-users, business intelligence
    role in project development, 113-14
    use in IMS design, 130-31
engineering, user-centred
    role, 7-8
'engineer-oriented' cultures
    characteristics, 16-18
    response to ease of use metrics
        adoption, 32-3, *33*
engineers, usability
    importance of understanding
        colleagues, 93-4
    personal qualities required, 59-61,
        192-3
    role, 1-2, 7-8
environments, organisational
    challenges, 16-20
    impact on efficiency, 9-10
    see also types eg. 'customer oriented';
        'design oriented'; 'engineer
        oriented'
evaluation, outcome
    strategy for successful relationships,
        96
experts, business intelligence
    lack as hindrance to project
        development, 113-14

FDA (Food and Drug Administration),
    63
'feature value analysis'
    role within project management,
        141-2
'feature/function analysis'

role within project management,
    142-4
feedback, project, 27-9
findings, project
    communication of, 117-21, *118, 120*
focus groups
    use in IMS design, 128-30, *129*
Food and Drug Administration (FDA),
    63

G2B (Government-to-Business)
    interaction initiative, 70
G2C (Government-to-Citizen)
    interaction initiative, 70, 71-2
G2G (Government-to-Government)
    interaction initiative, 70
goals and goal setting
    assessment of, 27-9
    need and usefulness, 25-7, 169-70
government, electronic
    barriers to successful delivery, 72-4
    definition (USA), 65
    drivers for extension of, 67-72, *68,*
        69
Government-to-Business (G2B)
    interaction initiative, 70
Government-to-Citizen (G2C)
    interaction initiative, 70, 71-2
Government-to-Government (G2G)
    interaction initiative, 70
governments, organisation of
    barrier to E-government delivery,
        72-3
groups, focus
    use in IMS design, 128-30, *129*

Hanson, K., 28, 33
Health and Human Services,
    Department of (USA)
    case study of web site redesign, 63-
        90, *68, 69, 77-8, 82, 83*
    organisation and structure, 63
hhs.gov/ web site
    barriers to successful delivery, 72-4

drivers for redesign, 67-72, *68, 69*
lessons from web redesign, 83-4
reason for redesign, 64-6
redesign process, 74-83, 84-7
Hofstede, G., 9, 192
Hura, S., 181
hypotheses, task
    role in project planning, 52-33

IAs (Information Architects)
    case study of role, 139-50, *141, 145,*
        148
    definition and characteristics, 135-7
    value to project management, 150-
        51
image, organisational
    importance of web site, 65
impasses, workplace
    case study, 96-110, *106*
    strategies for resolution, 105-110,
        106
    threat to web redesign success, 64
IMS (Information Map Studio) project
    challenges in development of,
        112-31, *118, 121, 124, 125, 127,*
        129
    definition and value, 111-12
    usability improvements at SAS, *118*
inertia, inter-organisational and per-
        sonal
    threat to web redesign, 89
information, reorganisation of
    process in web redesign, 80-82, *82*
Information Architects (IAs)
    case study of role, 139-50, *141, 145,*
        148
    definition and characteristics, 135-7
    value to project management, 150-
        51
Information Map Studio (IMS) project
    challenges in development of, 112-
        31, *118, 121, 124, 125, 127, 129*
    definition and value, 111-12
    usability improvements at SAS, *118*

Institutionalization of Usability
    (Schaeffer), 54
intelligence, business
    role of IMS, 111-12
interaction
    E-government initiatives (USA), 70
interactive voice response (IVR) systems
    case study of weakness correction,
        178-89, *183*
internet
    as source of IMS project end-users,
        114
internet, redesign
    case studies, 43-54, 63-90, *51, 68,*
        69, 77-8, 82, 83
    drivers for, 67-72, *68, 69*
    see also testing, iterative
Intuit
    case study of ease of use metrics
        adoption, *36*
IVR (interactive voice response) systems
    case study of weakness correction,
        178-89, *183*

JCPenney (retail company)
    web site redesign case study, 43-50

knowledge, domain
    barrier to IMS development, 121-5,
        124, 125

language, appropriate
    importance in conflict resolution,
        107
language, bureaucratic
    barrier to E-government delivery, 73
listening, inter-personal
    importance in conflict resolution,
        107

Mauro, C., 26
metrics, 'ease of use'
    adoption by organisations, 32-6, *33,*
        34, 36
    benefits, 23-31, *32*

characteristics, 21-3, *22, 23*
Molich, R., 181
Morville, L., 135
motivation, team
    role of 'ease of use' metrics, 25-6

National Adult Literacy Survey (USA),
    73
negotiation
    role within project management,
        144-5
Nielson, J., 181
Norman, D., 16-17

objectives, task
    role in project planning, 52-3
OLAP/cube data manipulation, 122
opinions, accommodation of
    importance in conflict resolution,
        108
organisations
    image as influence on web site
        design, 65
    impact of cultures on efficiency,
        9-10
    threats to web redesign, 87-90
    see also change, organisational;
        cultures, organisational;
        outcomes, organisational
outcomes, decision-making
    evaluation of, 96
outcomes, organisational
    necessity to meet, 169-70
outputs, business
    impact of organisational cultures,
        9-10

Peregrine Systems, 28-9
PICTIVE approach
    to IMS design, 122-3
pilot studies (project)
    experience at Siemens, 171
Placeware Web Conferencing, 117
planning, projects

importance of reflection, 95-6, *95*
need for budget planning, 138-9
role of objectives, 52-4
role of task hypotheses/objectives, 52-3
plans, sales, 42
PMA (President's Management Agenda)
in relation to E-government, 70
Polansky, A., 10
policies, web site
need for re-evaluation, 66
politics, inter-organisational
challenge for web redesign, 87-90
practitioners, user-centred design
importance of understanding colleagues, 93-4
personal qualities required, 59-61, 173-4, 192-3
role, 1-2, 7-8, 155-6, *156*
see also teams, user interface design
President's Management Agenda (PMA)
in relation to E-government, 70
prioritisation, causes and needs
within change projects, 56-7
prioritisation, work tasks, 26-7
problems, clarification
strategy for successful relationships, 96
processes, web site management
need for re-evaluation, 66
profiles, stereotypes
'Carl the Customer', 20
'Dana the Designer', 18-19
'Edward the Engineer', 17-18
'Project Parameter Matrix'
case study of use, 140-50, *141, 145, 148*
projects (work projects)
barriers to completion, 113-14, 137
case study of UCD management, 139-50, *141, 145, 148*
see also activities and tools eg budgets, project; communication, project

findings; feedback, project; pilot studies; planning, projects
see also players eg customers, business intelligence; information architects; teams, project management
prototyping, iterative
process in web redesign, 79-80

Radford-Davenport, J., 117
rapport
importance in conflict resolution, 106
recruitment
business consultants, 113-14
test participants, 57
reflection, personal
importance in successful relationships, 95-6, *95*
see also review, group
Rehabilitation Act, 1973 (USA), 71
relationships, workplace
strategies for success, 95-6, *95*
threats to successful relationships, 87-9
see also colleagues; conflicts, workplace; vendors
Remedy Software (case study)
'ease of use' metrics adoption, *33*
reports, usability test
value as decision-making tool, 120-21, *121*
resolve, individual
value in conflict resolution, 107-8
resources, task
allocation of, 29-30, *29*
review, group
user interface design process, 167-8
see also reflection, personal
Rosenfeld, L., 135

SAS Institute
case study of IMS project, 111-31, *118, 121, 124, 125, 127, 129*

satisfaction
    role of ease of use metrics, 21-3, *22,*
        23
Schaeffer, E., 54
schedules, project
    hindrance of, 114-17
    need for planning, 138-9, 147-8
schedules, sales, 42
searches, web site
    case study of redesign, 50-54, *51*
sensitivity, personal
    importance when effecting change,
        57
Siemens Medical Solutions (USA)
    case study of UI design, 154-75
    organisation and structure, 153-4
site maps
    function and detail, 145-6, *145, 146*
site-search (JCPenney)
    case study of web site redesign, 50-
        54, *51*
Six Sigma process insurance method
    case study of use, 36, 180-87, *183*
    characteristics, 179
software
    development cultures, 9-10
    development process, 5-7
    see also design, user-centred
specifications, user interface, 171-2
Spool, J., 41
stereotypes
    'Carl the Customer', 20
    'Dana the Designer', 18-19
    'Edward the Engineer', 17-18
studies, pilot
    experience at Siemens, 171
support, executive and operational
    pre-requisite for web redesign, 89-90
support and counsel, external
    importance in conflict resolution,
        108-9
systems, interactive voice response
        (IVR)

case study of weakness correction,
    178-89, *183*
tasks (work tasks)
    importance of prioritisation, 26-7
    role of objectives, 52-3
teams, project management
    role and organisation, 154-6, *155,*
        156
teams, user interface design
    membership, 156-9
testing, iterative
    process in web redesign, 79-80
tests, usability
    hindrance of time schedules, 114-17
    process in web redesign, 76-9, *77, 78*
    value of reports, 120-21, *121*
Thompson, T., 64-5
time, lack of
    barrier to IMS development, 114-17,
        125-31, *127, 129*
timetables, project
    hindrance of, 114-17
    need for planning, 138-9, 147-8
timetables, sales, 42
trust (personal)
    importance in conflict resolution,
        106
    see also distrust
Tudor, L., 122

UCD *see* design, user-centred
UI (user interface) design *see* design,
        user interface
usability, definition, 3
User Interface Specifications, 171-2
user-centred design *see* design, user-
        centred
user interface (UI) design *see* design,
        user interface
US Health and Human Services,
        Department of
    case study of web site redesign, 63-
        90, *68, 69, 77-8, 82, 83*

organisation and structure, 63

validation
    design process, 166-7
    role in organisational change, 58
vendors
    importance of relationship
        cultivation, 59-60
videos, editing of
    role in effecting organisational
        change, 58
viewpoints, accommodation of
    importance in conflict resolution,
        108

web sites, redesign

case studies, 43-54, 63-90, *51, 68,
    69, 77-8, 82, 83*
drivers for, 67-72, *68, 69*
see also testing, iterative
whiteboards
    use in design, 123-4, *124*, 126-8, *127*
wireframes
    use and value, 148-50, *148*
workplaces
    culture types *see* 'design oriented';
        'engineer oriented'
    see also conflicts, workplace;
        relationships, workplace
worldwide web
    as source of IMS project end-users,
        114

About the Authors

JEAN ANDERSON

Jean Anderson is a Senior User Interface Designer and Usability Analyst at Siemens Medical Solutions USA, Inc. Her current focus is on the challenges involved in designing web-based applications for outpatient clinical care. She has in the past also designed web-based applications for patient registration and hospital bed management.

WENDY CASTLEMAN

Wendy Castleman is Principal User Research Scientist at Intuit in Mountain View, CA. She is a cognitive psychologist who has over 14 years of research and teaching experience. She has developed robust processes and produced substantial increases in product usability in both large and small technology companies. Previously, Wendy worked as a user researcher at Remedy Software, Peregrine Systems, Motorola, Certive and Lucent. She also has taught several university-level courses in Human Factors, Human Learning and Cognition and Statistics and Research Methods. She received her Ph.D. from the University of Texas at Austin.

JULIE RADFORD-DAVENPORT

Julie Radford-Davenport is a User Interface Analyst with SAS Institute in Cary, North Carolina, where she is engaged in enhancing the user experience for business intelligence applications.

Prior to joining SAS, Julie was employed with AT&T as the Lead Usability Engineer for a variety of employee intranet sites and human resources systems. She was responsible for a wide variety of user-centred tasks, including usability testing of character-based, web and graphical user interfaces, interviewing users and subject matter experts, prototyping, and leading the user interface design efforts of content sites and transactional web applications.

Julie received her undergraduate degree from Old Dominion University in Norfolk, Virginia, and her Master's degree from Wake Forest University in Winston-Salem, North Carolina in 1993.

KAAREN HANSON

Kaaren Hanson is the Director of Customer Centered Development at Intuit, Inc. She is co-founder and President of the Bay Area Chapter of the Usability Professionals' Association (UPA). Before joining Intuit in 2002, Kaaren served as the Director of User Experience at Remedy Software and Peregrine Systems. Kaaren's trademark is developing user experience standards, coaching diverse teams to meet those standards, and measuring the effects of usability on behaviour and the bottom line. She received both her MA and Ph.D. from Stanford University.

FRANCIS (HANK) HENRY

Francis (Hank) Henry is the founder of Francis Henry Consulting, a Dallas-based independent user experience consultancy with a specialisation in B2C e-commerce. His 25-year retail merchandising career included stints at Montgomery Ward, The Limited, and JCPenney, where from 2000 to 2004 he managed jcpenney.com's Customer Experience Group and built their first usability lab.

As a usability professional, he has also worked with such firms as GSI Commerce, Creative Good, and Electronic Data Systems (EDS). Hank is active in the Usability Professionals' Association, having served on the conference committee for the past two years.

SUSAN L. HURA

Susan L. Hura, Ph.D. is the founder of SpeechUsability, a consultancy focusing on improving the user experience by incorporating user-centred design practices in speech technology projects. Susan founded the usability programme at

Intervoice as their Head of User Experience, and is a member of the Board of Directors of AVIOS. She received her Ph.D. from the University of Texas at Austin.

CONRAD MULLIGAN

Conrad Mulligan is a Senior Analyst with McNeil Technologies, Inc., a professional consulting firm based in Springfield, Virginia. He worked closely with the Department of Health and Human Services' usability and accessibility experts for several years where he provided project management, information design and technical writing services.

He was an integral member of the team that produced Research-Based Web Design and Usability Guidelines (http://usability.gov/pdfs/guidelines.html), a ground-breaking book of peer-reviewed and independently-ranked website design guidelines. Conrad has also authored or co-authored numerous papers and informal 'lessons learned' on accessibility and website design. He holds an M.Sc. from the London School of Economics.

ADAM POLANSKY

Adam Polansky has over 20 years' experience in media development and has been an information architect since 1997. He has led or contributed to the development of websites for such companies as Dr Pepper, Radio City Entertainment, American Express, AARP, Intel, Microsoft, Sabre, Corporate Express and Texas Instruments. Currently, he is Lead Information Architect at Travelocity.com.

A frequent speaker and guest lecturer, he holds a Bachelor of Science from the University of Texas and is a member of the IA Institute, the American Association of Information Science & Technology. He is also a Past President of the Dallas/Fort Worth Chapter of the Usability Professionals' Association.

ELIZABETH ROSENZWEIG

Elizabeth Rosenzweig is a Principal at Bubble Mountain Consulting, where she does user interface design, architecture and innovation, in addition to leadership training for her clients. Elizabeth is also a Research Scientist at the Media Lab at MIT, where she does research on voting technology.

Previously Elizabeth was a Principal Research Scientist at Eastman Kodak Company for 14 years, where she built the Boston Usability Lab – a usability-engineering centre of expertise – at the Kodak Boston Software Development Center in Lowell, Massachusetts. In addition to creating and running the lab, she was instrumental in defining and putting online the standards for graphical user interface design that are in use throughout Kodak.

Elizabeth has served on the Board of Directors of the Usability Professionals' Association since 1999, and was President during 2003–2004. She is the current Co-Director of Outreach. With 20 years of industry experience, Elizabeth frequently presents at national conferences and has been a contributor to professional journals.

PAUL SHERMAN

Paul Sherman is Director of User-Centered Design and Usability at Sage Software in Atlanta, GA. Prior to joining Sage he was a usability consultant. His projects included usability testing and interface design for IT applications, e-commerce websites, financial planning and portfolio management software applications, and telecommunications hardware and software applications. Before moving to Texas, Paul worked at Lucent Technologies in New Jersey, where he supervised the user interface design of several telecommunications management applications, and led efforts to develop cross-product user interface standards.

He received his Ph.D. in 1997 from the University of Texas at Austin. His research focused on how pilots' use of computers and automated systems on the flight deck affected their individual and team performance. While at UT-Austin, Paul logged over 145 flights observing pilots in the cockpit during commercial airline flight operations. Paul is also Vice-President of the Usability Professionals' Association (www.usabilityprofessionals.org), was the founding President of the UPA Dallas/Fort Worth Chapter, and is a Full Member of the Human Factors and Ergonomics Society.

MARY FRANCES THEOFANOS

Mary Frances Theofanos is a Computer Scientist in the Visualization and Usability Group in the Information Access Division of the National Institute of Standards and Technology where she is the programme manager of the Industry Usability Reporting (IUSR) Project and the Common Industry Format for Usability Test Reports, developing standards for usability. She is also working with the Biometrics Group evaluating usability of biometric systems. Previously, she was the Manager of the National Cancer Institute's (NCI) Communication Technologies Research Center (CTRC), a state-of-the-art usability testing facility for websites, applications, and emerging technologies, as well as a training facility and collaborative design centre, where she established an extensive research programme on the intersection of accessibility and usability.

Before joining NCI, Mary spent 15 years as a programme manager for software technology at the Oak Ridge National Laboratory complex of the US Department of Energy. A long-time member of both ACM and IEEE, Mary received her Bachelor's degree in mathematics from the University of Richmond and her Master's degree in computer science from the University of Virginia. She is currently a Ph.D. candidate in software engineering at George Mason University, working on her dissertation.

LESLIE G. TUDOR

Leslie G. Tudor received her Ph.D. in 1991 from Rutgers University in New Brunswick, New Jersey. Her research focused on both the psychology of perception and the mental transformation of three-dimensional ambiguous forms.

Upon graduating from Rutgers, Leslie worked at Bell Communications Research where she was mentored in various usability-based methodologies, and pioneered the Collaborative Analysis of Requirements and Design (CARD) method, which she still uses extensively. She worked for AT&T/Lucent Technologies Bell Labs for 8 years, where she was a Distinguished Member of Technical Staff. While at Bell Labs, she provided usability support to web, desktop, LCD and auditory interface projects, as well as to forward-looking physical design efforts.

Leslie is currently a Senior Software Manager of the Business Intelligence and Applications Usability Group at SAS Institute in Cary, North Carolina. At SAS, she manages a wonderful team of 15 usability engineers who work on various web- and desktop-based business intelligence products. A strong advocate of user-centred design methodologies, Leslie has conducted participatory design, contextual inquiry, and usability test sessions both domestically and abroad. She has also authored nine usability-based patents.

JOEL ZIFF

Joel Ziff, EdD, Ziff Consulting Group, Lesley University and Cambridge College, is a psychologist with 25 years' experience offering training, consultation and coaching to organisations, groups and individuals. Clients have included technology start-ups, non-profit organisations and health provider groups.

DIRK ZIMMERMANN

Dirk Zimmermann leads the User Interface Concept and Design Group for Clinical Systems at Siemens Medical Solutions USA, Inc. His current focus is on implementing and optimising user-centred design practices throughout the whole organisation and on migrating all current and new clinical systems to a standard UI paradigm.

He previously worked as a UI Design and Usability Engineering consultant for Siemens Business Services, where he was involved in both R&D and commercially focused projects within and outside Siemens.

Printed and bound by CPI Group (UK) Ltd, Croydon, CR0 4YY

01/11/2024

01782599-0004